food in jars

PRESERVING IN SMALL BATCHES
❧ YEAR-ROUND ❧

MARISA McCLELLAN

RUNNING PRESS
PHILADELPHIA · LONDON

Cover and interior design by Amanda Richmond
Edited by Kristen Green Wiewora
Typography: Rosewood, Clarendon, and Helvetica

Running Press Book Publishers
2300 Chestnut Street
Philadelphia, PA 19103-4371

Visit us on the web!
www.runningpresscooks.com

TO MY MOTHER, LEANA.

She is the reason I put food in jars.

CONTENTS

INTRODUCTION

WHEN I WAS FIRST LEARNING TO WALK, MY MOM and her best friend held a ceremony of sorts for my newly mobile self. They laid out a circle of objects. Paint brushes, musical instruments, a toy stethoscope, anything that could represent a future career. They then set me in the middle of the circle to let me explore. The hope was to discern a little about what I would become when I grew up. I grabbed a felt tip pen and a particularly well-worn wooden spoon and settled down to gnaw on my newly gotten treasures. They cheered and announced that I'd become a food writer someday. Much to everyone's delight, thirty-plus years later, that's exactly what I've become.

I grew up in a household that occasionally canned. Living in California and Oregon meant that during the summer, there was always an abundance of berries, plums, and apples. Two or three times a year, we'd go picking, gather windfall apples, or benefit from the benevolence of a friend with more fruit than time. My mom would pull out her largest stockpot and we'd pit, chop, mash, and simmer our way to half a dozen glowing jars of jam or fruit butter.

It wasn't until I was twenty-six that I started canning on my own. I was living in Philadelphia by then and one summer day, a friend and I went blueberry picking. When I got home, I did what felt natural. I made some jam. (Of course, I called my mom ten times during the process to consult.) With that single batch, I was well and truly bitten by the canning bug and had to do more. When I decided to start my own food blog, writing about canning and preserving just seemed like the right thing to do. I had no idea I was creating a career for myself as a canning teacher, writer, and all-around evangelist.

These days, I can because I love the process and the results. Once you start, there's really no going back flavor-wise to commercially made jams, chutneys, and pickles. It's also something of a deal. I like to compare it to the stock market practice of buying low and selling high: You get your produce at the peak of its season, when it's cheap, ripe, and delicious (that's the buying low part), invest a bit of time, and then enjoy the fruits of your labor all year round (sell high). In addition to the economic benefits, there's a great deal of joy and satisfaction to be had in knowing what goes into the food that you and your family eat.

This isn't to say that I'm encouraging people to go crazy and start preserving everything they eat. I certainly don't do that and it's not a reasonable expectation these days. However, I do suggest that you find one or two things that you love to eat and make those the items you focus your energies on. Specialize. Make a yearly habit of cooking up some strawberry jam, peach salsa, or a dozen pints of dilly beans. It's really all about what brings you joy.

GETTING STARTED: EQUIPMENT

Most people believe that you need a ton of special equipment in order to get canning. Truth is, provided your kitchen is stocked with some basics (I'm talking pots, bowls, and measuring cups here, not Viking stoves) you can do a wide variety of canning with what you've already got.

THE POTS

The first is a nice roomy pot for cooking your jam or bringing brine to a boil. I like to use either enameled cast iron or stainless steel (All-Clad makes an 8-quart stock pot that is perfection for jams, jellies and fruit butters, but any pot 6 to 10 quarts/5.7 to 9.5 liters in capacity will work). Make sure that you choose a nonreactive pot (no bare cast iron or untreated aluminum); otherwise, your finished product could end up with a metallic flavor. Know also that when it comes to the shape of your pot, wider is better. It increases the surface area of the jam and makes for shorter cooking times.

The second pot you want to have on hand is a small saucepan, for simmering the lids. Standard canning jars in the United States are three-part contraptions. You've got a jar, a ring (also known as a band), and the flat metal lid. There's a strip of sealing compound embedded in each and every lid that must be softened prior to use. To soften that compound, you simply simmer (try not to boil them if you can manage it) the lids in a small pan of water for ten or so minutes. Do remember that lids can only be used once for canning (if you soften a couple too many during canning prep, they can be used again. They just can't be sealed to a jar and then reused).

The last pot is your canning pot. A lot of people think they need to spend some bucks here and get themselves one of those speckly enameled pots with the specialized rack. Except I've found that after a couple of seasons, they start to rust and break down. Plus, who's got space for a huge pot that only serves one purpose?

I like to use my standard stock pot (it's made by Cuisinart and sells for about $60) with a small round cake cooling rack dropped in the bottom as my canning rig. Any large pot will work as a canning pot, as long as it's deep enough so that the jars are fully submerged with an inch of water covering them and you've still got a bit of room for the water to boil.

If you do choose to set up your own canning pot, don't skip the rack. It allows the boiling water to fully circulate and protects the jars from the direct heat of the burner, which in turn helps to prevent breakage.

OTHER TOOLS

In addition to your pots, it's helpful to have several measuring cups on hand. I like having a few larger-capacity heat-resistant (such as Pyrex) measuring cups around, as well as a stainless-steel 1-cup/250 ml measure (so handy for filling 1-pint/500 ml and half-pint/250 ml) jars.

As far as specialized canning tools go, there are two that I find particularly useful. The first is a wide-mouth funnel and the second is a jar lifter. While you don't *have* to have either of these tools, they will make your canning life significantly easier. The magnetic lid lift that comes in most canning tool kits is also nifty, but by no means essential.

Beyond that, there are a few tools that are nice to have that I will reference on occasion in these recipes. Included in that list are a sharp paring knife, a serrated-edge peeler, a Microplane zester, a candy thermometer, a splatter shield, a fine-mesh strainer, and an immersion blender.

THE WHYS OF PROCESSING PRESERVES

The bulk of the recipes included in this book are designed for boil-ing water bath canning. This is the process in which filled jars are submerged in a pot of boiling water and simmered for a prescribed amount of time. This is also the step that scares most people off from canning, as they think it is messy, time-consuming, or dangerous. But as with so many kitchen tasks, after you've done it once or twice, it will lose its intimidation factor.

It is important not to skip the boiling-water process, as it performs two tasks and does both exceedingly well. First, boiling the filled jars ensures than any contaminants that might have landed in your jars are killed (keep in mind that this processing method only works with high-acid foods. More about that in a minute). Second, it guarantees that there will be enough heat inside the jars that when you remove them from the water, the heat will rapidly escape, pulling any remaining air out of the jars and creating a solid, airtight seal. This is what keeps your jams, butters, and pickles fresh.

HOW TO PROCESS

1. If you're starting with brand-new jars, remove their lids and rings. If you're using older jars, check the rims to make sure there are no chips or cracks.

2. Put the rack into the canning pot and put the jars on top.

3. Fill the pot (and jars) with water to cover and bring to a boil. I have found that this is the very easiest way to heat up the jars in preparation for canning because you're going to have to heat up the canning pot anyway. Why not use that energy to heat up the jars as well?

4. Put the lids in a small saucepan, cover with water, and bring them to the barest simmer on the back of the stove.

5. While the canning pot comes to a boil, prepare your product.

6. When your recipe is complete, remove the jars from the canning pot (pouring the water back into the pot as you remove the jars) and set them on a clean towel on the counter. There's no need to invert them; the jars will be so hot that any remaining water will rapidly evaporate. Remove the lids with tongs or a magnetic lid wand and lay them out on the clean towel.

7. Carefully fill the jars with your product. Depending on the recipe, you'll need to leave between $\frac{1}{4}$ and $\frac{1}{2}$ inch/6 mm and 12 mm of headspace (that's the room between the surface of the product and the top of the jar). Jams and jellies typically get $\frac{1}{4}$ inch/6 mm, while thicker products and pickles get $\frac{1}{2}$ inch/12 mm.

8. Wipe the rims of the jar with a clean, damp paper towel or the edge of a clean kitchen towel. If the product you're working with is very sticky, you can dip the edge of the cloth in distilled white vinegar for a bit of a cleaning boost.

9. Apply the lids and screw the bands on the jars to hold the lids down during processing. Tighten the bands with the tips of your fingers to ensure that they aren't overly tight. This is known as "fingertip tight."

introduction | 11

10. Carefully lower the filled jars into the canning pot. You may need to remove some water as you put the jars in the pot. A heat-resistant measuring cup is the best tool for this job, as it won't transfer heat to your hand.

11. Once the pot has returned to a rolling boil, start your timer. The length of the processing time will vary from recipe to recipe.

12. When your timer goes off, promptly remove the jars from the water bath. Gently place them back on the towel-lined countertop and let them cool.

13. The jar lids should begin to ping soon after they've been removed from the pot. The pinging is the sound of the seals forming; the center of the lids will become concave as the vacuum seal takes hold.

14. After the jars have cooled for 24 hours, remove the bands and check the seals. You do this by grasping the jar by the edges of the lid and gently lifting it an inch or two off the countertop. The lid should hold fast.

15. Once you've determined that your seals are good, you can store your jars in a cool, dark place (with the rings off, please) for up to a year. Any jars with bad seals can still be used — just store them in the refrigerator and use within 2 weeks.

GAUGING A JAM'S SET

Your first few jamming forays may feel like guesswork, but after the first few batches you'll start to see the signs of doneness more clearly.

1. When jam starts to cook, it just looks like bits of fruit bobbing around in thin syrup. The bubbles will be foamy and the boil easy to stir down.

2. Monitoring the temperature is a helpful way to track the progress of your cooking: jam sets at 220°F/105°C.

3. One of my favorite ways to check for doneness is by using the sheet test. Watch the jam as it drips off the back of a spoon. If the drips are thin and quick-moving, the jam still has a way to go (see the photo on the left, above). If they run together and form a sheet as they drip down the spoon, set has been achieved (right, above).

4. If you're feeling uncertain about your set after you've filled all your jars, take a peek at the remnants of jam in your canning pot. If it sticks and sets to the side of the pan, take heart! The jam should eventually set in the jars as well: give it about 2 weeks.

HIGH ACID VS. LOW ACID

In the course of learning to can and then sharing my excitement about it, I've heard so many people confess their canning fears. Mostly, they're terrified that they are going to kill their families. Hear me now. If you stick to the high-acid foods—like most jams, jellies, and pickles—you are not going to kill anyone.

Botulism is the singular killer when it comes to canned goods, but it cannot grow in high-acid environments. This means that you'll never hear of a case of botulism having grown in a jar of strawberry jam or dill pickles. If something goes wrong with your high-acid foods, you will be able to tell immediately upon opening the jar. There will be a foul smell, colorful growth, or bubbling where there ought not be (and these things happen very rarely if you're following proper canning procedure).

There are a few varieties of fruit that exist in the very narrow gray area between high acid and low. These items need to be acidified to be canned safely and should be treated with care. This list includes figs, white peaches, Asian pears, bananas, mangoes, watermelon, and tomatoes (we'll get more in depth about how to safely can tomatoes in that section of the book). Take care when working with these fruits and always consult trusted recipe sources like the *Ball Blue Book* and the National Center for Home Food Preservation.

Most low-acid foods can be preserved safely at home with the help of a pressure canner (page 228).

COOKING TIMES

In most of these recipes, I've included suggested cooking times. However, these are just ranges and are not ironclad, particularly when it comes to jams, jellies, and marmalades. Cooking times can vary depending on the humidity in the air, the moisture level in the fruit, the width of your pot and the intensity of your stove's heat. It's important to use your judgment when cooking up these sweet preserves and not just depend solely on the suggested cooking times. Monitoring temperature (see page 13) or using the saucer test (see page 77) are two good ways to know when the jam is really ready to come off the heat.

YIELDS

Just like cooking times, the yields on these recipes can vary. I have tested and retested the recipes to ensure that they work, but there are a number of factors that can nudge the final amount up or down a few ounces. One particular culprit is a rainy growing season. Lots of precipitation can cause fruits to take on more water while on the plant. This means that during cooking, there will be more liquid that has to be evaporated out of the fruit, leading to smaller yields. Conversely, during hotter, dryer years, the fruit can become intense with sugar (this is why dry-farmed tomatoes and strawberries are so magically delicious) and can yield slightly more product.

ADJUSTING FOR ALTITUDE

One of the quirks of life on earth is that as you increase your elevation, the temperature at which water boils decreases. With every reduction in degree, you lose a bit of bacteria-killing power. If you live between sea level and 1,000 feet, you don't have to make any adjustments and can use the recipes as written. However, for additional altitude, you must add time to the processing step.

1,001 to 3,000 feet	add 5 minutes
3,001 to 6,000 feet	add 10 minutes
6,001 to 8,000 feet	add 15 minutes
8,001 to 10,000 feet	add 20 minutes

From left to right: Blackberry, Apple-Cranberry, Cantaloupe Vanilla, Sour Cherry, Damson Plum

JAMS

WHEN IT COMES TO CANNING, MY FIRST LOVE will always be jam. There's a certain art and alchemy that takes place when you combine fruit, sugar, and heat that keeps me coming back, season after season.

This doesn't mean that every batch of jam I make is perfect. I've made some jam so firmly set that the knife seems to bounce right off (a small batch of rhubarb jam immediately springs to mind) as well as some that are so runny that the jars slosh when rattled. When that happens, I just call it syrup and tell everyone that I meant to make it like that. Most of the time they believe me.

What's more, every season is a little bit different. Really wet springs can produce strawberries so watery that getting anything beyond juice is a victory and a really hot June will have the blueberries ready for picking a full two weeks early. Don't get complacent and learn to appreciate the variable bounty.

Remember, jam is good for so much more than just smearing on your morning toast or adding to a peanut butter sandwich. Spoon a few dollops into vinaigrette for a fruit-infused salad dressing. Brush a bit on chicken or pork for an instant glaze.

Some of the following recipes call for pectin and some do not. In the recipes that do call for it, they all specify liquid pectin. I prefer a loose-set jam over one that is super firm and I've found that I can best get that consistency with liquid pectin.

For the recipes that do not call for pectin at all, I do recommend that you get yourself a candy thermometer so that you can track the temperature of the jam as it cooks. Jam reaches its set point at 220°F/105°C, so as long as you're able to cook it to that temperature, you should be able to avoid total syrupiness. I use an old-fashioned candy thermometer because it doesn't require batteries and is much harder to break than the electronic ones.

Keep in mind that regular jam is absolutely dependent on sugar to achieve a good set, particularly if you're working without additional pectin. If you've ever made candy at home, you'll know how sugar passes through different consistencies as you cook it to ever-higher temperatures. Jam achieves its set point at 220°F/105°C, which in candy making is known as the jelly stage. If you reduce the amount of sugar, you make it harder (or even impossible) for the jam to reach that temperature and achieve set.

If you really want to make reduced- or no-sugar jams, I suggest you look into Pomona's Pectin. It achieves set through a different array of reactions than traditional pectins do. Alternatively, you could also check out the fruit butter section of this book (page 51), which features a number of low-sugar fruit spreads.

VANILLA-RHUBARB JAM
WITH EARL GREY

THIS WAS ONE OF THE VERY FIRST JAMS I MADE that wasn't berry based and I liked it so much that I've made it many times since. In the beginning, the addition of the Earl Grey tea was simply a move to use up the end of a pot, but I find the hint of bergamot flavor it adds is quite nice. However, if you're not a fan, feel free to sub in a different kind of tea or even just water.

MAKES 4 (1-PINT/500 ML) JARS

8 cups chopped rhubarb
(about 3 pounds/1.4 kg rhubarb stalks)
4 cups/800 g granulated sugar
1 cup/240 ml double-strength brewed Earl Grey tea
1 vanilla bean, split and scraped
Juice of 1 lemon
Pinch salt
1 (3-ounce/85 ml) packet liquid pectin

Prepare a boiling water bath and 4 regular-mouth 1-pint/500 ml jars according to the process on page 10. Place the lids in a small saucepan, cover them with water, and simmer over very low heat.

In a large, nonreactive pot, combine the rhubarb, sugar, and tea and bring to a boil. Add the vanilla bean and seeds, lemon juice, and salt to the pot and let the mixture bubble gently over medium-high heat for 15 to 20 minutes, stirring regularly, until the rhubarb has broken down.

Add the packet of liquid pectin and increase the heat to high, to bring the jam up to a rolling boil. Let the jam boil vigorously for 3 to 4 minutes, stirring frequently to prevent the bottom from burning.

Remove the pot from the heat and ladle the jam into the prepared jars. Wipe the rims, apply the lids and rings, and process in a boiling water bath for 10 minutes (see page 11).

RHUBARB JAM

WITH STRAWBERRIES AND ORANGES

AT THE END OF A COLD WINTER, THERE'S LITTLE that makes me happier that the arrival of rhubarb. It means that spring is close (even if the mercury hasn't gotten the message yet). Some years I wait until the local strawberries arrive to make this jam, others I cheat and use frozen. Obviously, you get the best flavor from the local ones, but after a Northeast winter, it's hard not to want to jump the gun a little. For those of you fond of strawberry rhubarb pie, this jam is a nice substitute.

MAKES 5 (1-PINT/500 ML) JARS

6 cups chopped rhubarb
  (about 2½ pounds/1 kg rhubarb stalks)
4 cups chopped strawberries
  (about 2 dry pints/715 g strawberries)
Zest and juice of 2 oranges
5 cups/1 kg granulated sugar
1 teaspoon ground cinnamon
2 (3-ounce/85 ml) packets liquid pectin

Prepare a boiling water bath and 5 regular-mouth 1-pint/500 ml jars according to the process on page 10. Place the lids in a small saucepan, cover them with water, and simmer over very low heat.

In a large, nonreactive pot, combine the rhubarb, strawberries, orange zest and juice, sugar, and cinnamon and stir to incorporate. Bring to a boil and reduce heat to a simmer.

Let the fruit cook over medium-high heat (you want bubbles but not a vigorous boil) for approximately 15 to 20 minutes, until the rhubarb breaks down (if there are a few pieces here and there, it's okay, just as long as they are soft enough to break down with the back of a wooden spoon) and the jam has developed a glossy shine.

Add the pectin and increase the heat to high, letting the jam boil vigorously for 5 minutes. Remove the pot from the heat and ladle the jam into the prepared jars. Wipe the rims, apply the lids and rings, and process in a boiling water bath for 10 minutes (see page 11).

STRAWBERRY VANILLA JAM

EVERYONE THINKS THEY KNOW WHAT STRAWBERRY jam tastes like. That is, until they make it from scratch, with thoroughly red berries that were bred for flavor instead of an ability to travel. Truly, the homemade version is toe-curlingly good. Getting a good set out of strawberry jam is hard because there's not much in the way of natural pectin in these berries. However, if your finished product turns out to be closer to syrup than jam, don't apologize for it. Simply call it strawberry preserves and tell everyone it's exactly as you intended it to be. No one will be the wiser. You should also note that this jam calls a maceration period before cooking. This helps draw the juices out of the fruit and makes for a more luscious jam.

MAKES 4 (1-PINT/500 ML) JARS

8 cups hulled and chopped ripe strawberries
  (about 2 dry quarts/1.4 kg strawberries)
5 cups/1 kg granulated sugar, divided
2 vanilla beans, split and scraped
Zest and juice of 2 lemons
2 (3-ounce/85 ml) packets liquid pectin

In a nonreactive bowl, combine the chopped strawberries with 1 cup/200g of the sugar and the vanilla bean seeds and pods. Let the mixture sit at room temperature until the sugar begins to pull the liquid out of the berries, about 15 to 30 minutes, then cover and refrigerate overnight. If you don't want to wait overnight (or don't have the refrigerator space), even just 1 hour of maceration is better than none at all.

When you're ready to make the jam, prepare a boiling water bath and 4 regular-mouth 1-pint/500 ml jars according to the process on page 10. Place the lids in a small saucepan, cover them with water, and simmer over very low heat.

Remove the macerated strawberries from the refrigerator and pour everything into a large, nonreactive pot. Add the remaining 4 cups/800 g of sugar and lemon zest and juice and stir to combine. Bring to a boil over high heat (this jam will foam madly) and cook on high heat for 15 to 20 minutes, stirring regularly, until it takes on a thick, syrupy consistency.

(continued)

Remove the vanilla bean pods from the mixture. If you have an immersion blender, use it at this point to purée some of the fruit. Alternatively, transfer about a third of the jam to a blender and purée, then return puréed fruit to pot.

Add the pectin to the fruit mixture and bring to a rolling boil. Insert your candy thermometer into the jam and attach it to the side of the pot. Let the jam boil vigorously until it reaches 220°F/105°C.

Once the jam reaches 220°F/105°C and remains at that temperature for 2 minutes, remove the pot from the heat and ladle the jam into the prepared jars, leaving ½ inch headspace. Wipe the rims, apply the lids and rings, and process in a boiling water bath for 10 minutes (see page 11).

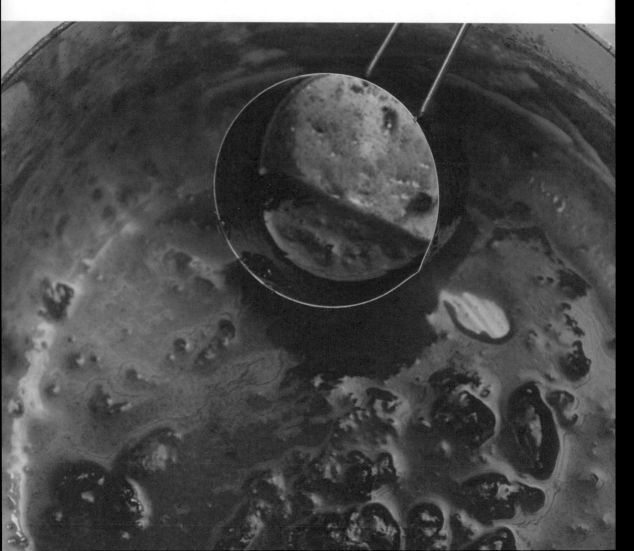

APRICOT JAM

APRICOT WAS NOT PART OF MY CHILDHOOD REPER-
toire of jams. When it came to homemade jams, we were more of a
plum and blueberry crowd. So I never gave it much thought until
the day someone introduced me to the company "We Love Jam" and their
Blenheim apricot jam, and it blew my preserve-lovin' mind. While I can't get
those precious Blenheims where I live, I've found that just about any locally
grown, tree-ripened apricot makes stellar jam and I can't really see going a
year without its sweet-tart goodness for spreading on buttered toast.

MAKES 3 (1 PINT/500 ML) JARS

6 cups pitted and diced apricots
  (about 3 pounds/1.4 kg whole apricots)
3$\frac{1}{2}$ cups/700 g granulated sugar
Zest and juice of 1 lemon

Prepare a boiling water bath and 3 regular-mouth 1-pint/500 ml jars according to the
process on page 10. Place the lids in a small saucepan, cover them with water, and
simmer over very low heat.

Combine the apricots and sugar in a large pot and bring to a boil over medium-high
heat. Boil for 10 to 15 minutes, until the fruit is tender and the liquid looks syrupy.

Add the lemon juice and zest and return to a boil. Insert your candy thermometer
into the jam and attach it to the side of the pot. Let the jam boil vigorously until it
reaches 220°F/105°C.

When the jam has reached 220°F/105°C and the temperature has remained steady
for 2 minutes, remove the pot from the heat and ladle the jam into the prepared jars.
Wipe the rims, apply the lids and rings, and process in a boiling water bath for 10 minutes (see page 11).

SOUR CHERRY JAM

IBELIEVE THAT SOUR CHERRY JAM WAS THE ORIGINAL
inspiration for those little rolls of Sweet Tarts that we all ate as kids.
Also known as tart or pie cherries, sour cherries are bright, tangy (but
not sour exactly, just perfectly piquant) and, when combined with a bit of
sugar and cooked into jam (or baked in a pie), they walk the line between
pleasantly sweet and achingly puckery. They are hard to find commercially, but tend to make appearances at farmers' markets in June or July.
Keep your eyes peeled and when you find them, make this jam.

MAKES 3 (1-PINT/500 ML) JARS

6 cups pitted and mashed sour cherries
  (about 3 pounds/1.4 kg whole cherries)
3 cups/600 g granulated sugar
1 (3-ounce/85 ml) packet liquid pectin

Prepare a boiling water bath and 3 regular-mouth 1-pint/500 ml jars according to the
process on page 10. Place the lids in a small saucepan, cover them with water, and
simmer over very low heat.

Combine the cherries and sugar in a large pot. Bring to a boil over high heat and let
it bubble for a good 20 minutes, occasionally skimming the foam from the surface of
the fruit as it develops. Add the pectin and boil for another 5 minutes. You want to
cook it until the bubbles are thick and look like molten lava.

Remove the pot from the heat and ladle the jam into the prepared jars. Wipe the
rims, apply the lids and rings, and process in a boiling water bath for 10 minutes (see
page 11).

Note: I love the taste of sour cherries, so I don't add a drop of extra flavor to this
jam. However, you might like to spice things up with ground cinnamon, nutmeg, cardamom, vanilla, or orange zest or juice (or anything else).

SPICED PLUM JAM

I SPENT THE FIRST NINE YEARS OF MY LIFE LIVING IN Southern California. I took backyard citrus and homegrown guava for granted. I also never truly valued the many plums that grew like magic in our yard each spring. They had deeply tart skins and juicy purple insides and made the best jam. Now that I live in a very urban neighborhood of Philadelphia, the fact that we once had access to such easy bounty seems like a miracle. I make at least one batch of this spiced plum jam each year, to help me remember those days.

MAKES 4 (1-PINT/500 ML) JARS

8 cups pitted and finely chopped plums
   (about 4 pounds/1.8 kg whole plums)
3$\frac{1}{2}$ cups/700 g granulated sugar
Zest and juice of 1 lemon
2 teaspoons ground cinnamon
$\frac{1}{2}$ teaspoon freshly grated nutmeg
$\frac{1}{4}$ teaspoon ground cloves
2 (3-ounce/85 ml) packets liquid pectin

Prepare a boiling water bath and 4 regular-mouth 1-pint/500 ml jars according to the process on page 10. Place the lids in a small saucepan, cover them with water, and simmer over very low heat.

Combine the plums and sugar in a large pot. Stir so that the plums begin to release their juice and mingle with the sugar. Bring to a boil and add the lemon zest and juice, cinnamon, nutmeg, and cloves. Let the jam continue to cook over high heat for 15 to 20 minutes, until it looks molten and really syrupy.

Add the pectin and bring to a rolling boil for a full 5 minutes. When it is done, it will look thick and shiny.

Remove the pot from the heat and ladle the jam into the prepared jars. Wipe the rims, apply the lids and rings, and process in a boiling water bath for 10 minutes (see page 11).
Note: I call for chopped plums in this recipe. However, if your plums are too ripe for regular chopping, just give them a big squeeze with your hands, pull the skin apart a little, and pluck out the pits.

PEACH JAM

EVERY SUMMER, I BUY MY WEIGHT IN PEACHES. Peaches have become one of those fruits that are nearly always available, but they are only transcendent during the months of July and August. Those mealy, impenetrable fruits that you pay a small fortune for during the winter can't possibly compare. Make this jam during the season and forget those out-of-season abominations.

MAKES 3 (1-PINT/500 ML) JARS

5 cups peeled, pitted, and chopped peaches
   (about 3 pounds/1.4 kg whole peaches)
3 cups/600 g granulated sugar
Zest and juice of 1 lemon
1 teaspoon ground cinnamon
½ teaspoon freshly grated nutmeg
1 (3-ounce/85 ml) packet liquid pectin

Prepare a boiling water bath and 3 regular-mouth 1-pint/500 ml jars according to the process on page 10. Place the lids in a small saucepan, cover them with water, and simmer over very low heat.

Combine the peaches and sugar in a large, nonreactive pot. Stir so that the peaches begin to release their juice and mingle with the sugar. Bring to a boil and add the lemon zest and juice, cinnamon, and nutmeg. Let the jam continue to cook over high heat for 15 to 20 minutes.

If you like a smoother jam, use an immersion blender (taking care not to burn yourself with hot jam) to break down some of the chunks. Add the pectin and bring to a rolling boil for a full 5 minutes. It should look thick and spreadable.

Remove the pot from the heat and ladle the jam into the prepared jars. Wipe the rims, apply the lids and rings, and process in a boiling water bath for 10 minutes (see page 11).

Note: When it comes to peeling peaches, most instructions will tell you to blanch and peel them whole. I've found that it's easier and less damaging to the fruit if you slice them in half and remove the pits prior to their hot-water dip. After 60 seconds in a pot of boiling water, the skin should easily pull away from the peach halves.

PEACH-PLUM-GINGER JAM

THIS PARTICULAR RECIPE WAS BORN BECAUSE I had a couple of pounds of peaches and plums that were ripening faster than I could eat them. A generous hunk of ginger was hanging out in the fruit bowl. The result is sweet and spicy and certainly not for the ginger-shy. It's a delight on toast, but even more miraculous baked on chicken or stirred together with some toasted sesame oil for a quick stir-fry sauce. Because this recipe doesn't use additional pectin, you can adapt it to the amount of fruit you have that needs to be used. However, when you don't use pectin, it's important to gauge the doneness of your jam using a candy thermometer or the saucer test (described on page 77).

MAKES 3 (1-PINT/500 ML) JARS

4 cups peeled, pitted, and mashed peaches
(about 2 pounds/910 g whole peaches)

2 cups pitted and mashed plums
(about 1 pound/ 455 g whole plums)

3 cups/600 g granulated sugar

$\frac{1}{2}$ cup/120 ml ginger juice (see note)

Prepare a boiling water bath and 3 regular-mouth 1-pint/500 ml jars according to the process on page 10. Place the lids in a small saucepan, cover them with water, and simmer over very low heat.

Combine all ingredients in a large pot. Bring to a simmer. Insert a candy thermometer into the jam and attach it to the side of the pot. Increase the heat and let the jam boil vigorously until it reaches 220°F/105°C.

When the jam has reached 220°F/105°C and the temperature has remained steady for 2 minutes, remove the pot from the heat and ladle the jam into the prepared jars.

Wipe the rims, apply the lids and rings, and process in a boiling water bath for 10 minutes (see page 11).

Note: To make ginger juice, shred a 4-ounce/115 g hunk of peeled fresh ginger in a blender or food processor with $\frac{1}{4}$ cup/60 ml of water. Pour the ginger pulp into a cheesecloth-lined sieve and squeeze out the liquid. Discard the remaining ginger pulp.

SWEET CHERRY-PLUM JAM

THOUGH I LOVE EATING SWEET CHERRIES WHEN they're ripe and in season, I've found that they don't make the best jam on their own. With their assertive sweetness, they run the risk of becoming akin to cough syrup in a preserve. But on a whim last summer, I tried cutting them with some tart plums and immediately knew I'd hit pay dirt. The plums give just the right amount of tart balance to the cherries and transform them into a true treat.

MAKES 4 (1-PINT/500 ML) JARS

3 cups pitted and chopped plums
(about 1$\frac{1}{2}$ pounds/680 g whole plums)
4 cups pitted and chopped sweet cherries
(about 2 pounds/910 g whole cherries)
3$\frac{1}{2}$ cups/700 g granulated sugar
Zest and juice of 1 lemon
2 (3-ounce/85 ml) packets liquid pectin

Prepare a boiling water bath and 4 regular-mouth 1-pint/500 ml jars according to the process on page 10. Place the lids in a small saucepan, cover them with water, and simmer over very low heat.

Combine the plums, cherries, and sugar in a large pot. Bring to a boil over high heat and cook for approximately 15 to 20 minutes, until the jam looks molten and syrupy.

Add the lemon zest and juice and the pectin. Bring to a rolling boil and boil for 5 minutes.

Remove the pot from the heat and ladle the jam into the prepared jars. Wipe the rims, apply the lids and rings, and process in a boiling water bath for 10 minutes (see page 11).

NECTARINE-LIME JAM

WHEN IT COMES TO SUMMERTIME PRESERVING, most people choose peaches over nectarines. However, I find that nectarines make amazing jams and have a distinct advantage over peaches: no need to peel! In this preserve, I've paired smooth nectarines with a whole heck of a lot of lime juice and zest, for a really tasty sweet and puckery spread. Stir a few spoonfuls into some oil and vinegar to make a light vinaigrette.

MAKES 3 (1-PINT/500 ML) JARS

5 cups pitted and chopped nectarines
   (about 3 pounds/1.4 kg whole nectarines)
3 cups/600 g granulated sugar
Zest and juice of 2 limes
1 (3-ounce/85 ml) packet liquid pectin

Prepare a boiling water bath and 3 regular-mouth 1-pint/500 ml jars according to the process on page 10. Place the lids in a small saucepan, cover them with water, and simmer over very low heat.

Combine the peaches and sugar in a large pot. Bring to a boil and let jam boil for 15 to 20 minutes over high heat, until the fruit softens and can be mashed with the back of a wooden spoon.

If you prefer a smoother-textured jam, use an immersion blender (taking care not to burn yourself with hot jam) to break down some of the chunks. If you prefer a chunkier jam, just leave it as is. Add the lime zest and juice and stir well. Add the pectin and bring to a rolling boil for a full 5 minutes, until it looks molten and syrupy.

Remove the pot from the heat and ladle the jam into the prepared jars. Wipe the rims, apply the lids and rings, and process in a boiling water bath for 10 minutes (see page 11).

SIMPLE RASPBERRY JAM

CONSIDER RASPBERRIES TO BE THE MOST PRECIOUS of the summer fruit. Each year, it takes an act of will to put aside enough for a batch of jam. I never regret the sacrifice after the fact though, as I do love having a couple of pints tucked away for the snowy days in February. Unlike the recipe for Nearly Seedless Blackberry-Sage Jam, I do not seed the fruit for this jam. I enjoy the gentle crunch of the raspberry seeds and actually find the jam somewhat less charming when they're absent. However, if you're a seed hater, feel free to seed (check out the instructions on page 37).

MAKES 3 (1-PINT/500 ML) JARS

6 cups crushed raspberries (about 2 dry quarts/980 g)
4 cups/800 g granulated sugar
Juice of 1 lemon
1 (3-ounce/85 ml) packet liquid pectin

Prepare a boiling water bath and 3 regular-mouth 1-pint/500 ml jars according to the the process on page 10. Place the lids in a small saucepan, cover them with water, and simmer over very low heat.

Combine the crushed berries and sugar in a large pot and stir to combine. Bring to a boil over high heat and stir frequently until all the berries have broken down and the bubbles look thick and viscous, about 15 to 20 minutes. Add the lemon juice and the pectin. Return to a rapid boil and allow the mixture to boil for about 5 minutes.

Remove the pot from the heat and ladle the jam into the prepared jars. Wipe the rims, apply the lids and rings, and process in a boiling water bath for 10 minutes (see page 11).

SMALL BATCH
MIXED STONE FRUIT JAM

HAVE YOU EVER FOUND YOURSELF IN A SCENARIO where the summer fruit you bought to eat out of hand is suddenly going much riper far faster than you can manage? You don't want to let it go to waste, but you can't devote the time to making something with it just now. That's when a small batch recipe like this comes in handy. Carve up a few of the ripest pieces of stone fruit, mix them with some sugar, and come back (up to 2 days) later when you can handle half an hour at the stove. The maceration time helps get the juices running and makes for very tasty jam (if you're a vanilla freak like me, toss half a vanilla bean in with the fruit for an infusion of vanilla flavor).

MAKES 3 (HALF-PINT/250 ML) JARS

3 cups pitted and chopped stone fruit (use any combination of peaches, plums, nectarines, pluots, or even cherries; about 1 ½ pounds/680 g mixed fruit)

2 cups/400 g granulated sugar

Zest and juice of 1 lemon

Combine the chopped fruit and sugar in an airtight container and place in the refrigerator for 2 to 48 hours.

When you're ready to make jam, prepare a boiling water bath and 3 half-pint/250 ml jars according to the process on page 10. Place the lids in a small saucepan, cover them with water, and simmer over very low heat.

Pour the macerated fruit into a medium pot. Bring to a boil and let the jam bubble, stirring regularly, until it reduces and develops a syrupy look.

Insert your candy thermometer into the jam and attach it to the side of the pot. Let the jam boil vigorously until it reaches 220°F/105°C.

When the jam has reached 220°F/105°C and the temperature remains steady for 2 minutes, remove the pot from the heat and ladle the jam into prepared jars. Wipe the rims, apply the lids and rings, and process in a boiling water bath for 10 minutes (see page 11).

NEARLY SEEDLESS
BLACKBERRY SAGE JAM

DURING MY CHILDHOOD IN PORTLAND, OREGON, I got very used to the idea of free blackberries. They grow wild all over the Pacific Northwest, to the point of becoming a nuisance (my father once had to rent a backhoe in order to reclaim a portion of our yard from the blackberry brambles). Those wild blackberries are *very* seedy, thus my habit of making seedless blackberry jam. If you prefer your blackberry jam to retain some crunch, feel free to skip the seeding step.

MAKES 3 (1-PINT/500 ML) JARS

6 cups seedless blackberry pulp (from 3 quarts/1.7 kg
   blackberries, mashed through a strainer with the back
   of a wooden spoon)

4 cups/800 g granulated sugar

15 to 20 fresh sage leaves

Zest and juice of 1 lemon

1 (3-ounce/85 ml) packet liquid pectin

Prepare a boiling water bath and 3 regular-mouth 1-pint/500 ml jars according to the process on page 10. Place the lids in a small saucepan, cover them with water, and simmer over very low heat.

In a large pot, combine the fruit pulp and sugar and bring to a boil over high heat. Add the sage leaves and lemon zest and juice and stir to combine. Let the mixture continue to boil, stirring frequently to prevent it from bubbling over.

When the mixture appears to have thickened, which should take approximately 20 to 25 minutes, reduce the heat to a simmer and add the pectin. Return to a boil for at least 5 minutes.

Remove the pot from the heat and ladle the jam into the prepared jars. Wipe the rims, apply the lids and rings, and process in a boiling water bath for 10 minutes (see page 11).

CANTALOUPE JAM ⌐ 2 ⌐

WITH VANILLA

CANTALOUPE IS NOT THE FIRST FRUIT THAT SPRINGS to mind when a canner's thoughts turn to jam. However, for the melon lovers in the crowd, I beg you not to skip this one. When you combine cantaloupe with a bit of sugar and vanilla, it ends up tasting like the best and most exotic Creamsicle you've ever had. As a Creamsicle lover, I find this feature highly enticing. By design, this recipe makes a fairly small batch. I find that one smallish melon or half of an enormous one yields just the right amount.

MAKES 3 (HALF-PINT/250 ML) JARS

$2\frac{1}{2}$ cups chopped peeled cantaloupe
   (from about 2 pounds/910 g cantaloupe)
$1\frac{1}{2}$ cups/300 g granulated sugar
1 vanilla bean, split and scraped
Zest of 1 lemon
1 tablespoon bottled lemon juice
1 (3-ounce/85 ml) packet liquid pectin

Prepare a boiling water bath and 3 half-pint/250 ml jars according to the process on page 10. Place the lids in a small saucepan, cover them with water, and simmer over very low heat.

Combine the cantaloupe, sugar, and vanilla bean pod and seeds in a nonreactive pot. Bring to a boil over high heat and cook for 8 to 10 minutes.

Add the lemon zest, lemon juice, and the packet of liquid pectin. Return to a vigorous boil. Cook for an additional 3 to 4 minutes, until the bubbles look thick. Remove the vanilla bean pod and discard.

Remove the pot from the heat and ladle the jam into the prepared jars. Wipe the rims, apply the lids and rings, and process in a boiling water bath for 10 minutes (see page 11).

BLUEBERRY JAM

WHEN IT COMES TO CANNING, BLUEBERRIES WERE my gateway fruit (although they didn't usher me through the doorway into total canning preoccupation until I reached adulthood). Growing up, I'd often pick them with my family, but I always left the jam making and canning to my mom, participating only when it came time to squish the berries into jammable shape with my fingers (there's something so deeply satisfying about crushing those juicy little blue orbs into pulpy bits).

MAKES 3 (1-PINT/500 ML) JARS

6 cups smashed blueberries
   (about 3 quarts/1.7 kg whole blueberries)
4 cups/800 g granulated sugar
Zest and juice of 1 lemon
2 teaspoons ground cinnamon
1/2 teaspoon freshly grated nutmeg
2 (3-ounce/85 ml) packets liquid pectin

Prepare a boiling water bath and 3 regular-mouth 1-pint/500 ml jars according to the process on page 10. Place the lids in a small saucepan, cover them with water, and simmer over very low heat.

Combine the smashed blueberries and sugar in a large pot. Bring to a boil over high heat and add the lemon zest and juice, cinnamon, and nutmeg and cook for about 15 to 20 minutes, stirring frequently, until the jam is shiny and thick looking. Add the pectin and return to a rolling boil for a full 5 minutes.

Remove the pot from the heat and ladle the jam into the prepared jars. Wipe the rims, apply the lids and rings, and process in a boiling water bath for 10 minutes (see page 11).

Note: It's important to mash your berries before combining them with sugar and putting them in the pot. Without the juice from inside the blueberries, the sugar won't break down as quickly and could easily scorch before it has a chance to dissolve.

DAMSON PLUM JAM

TO ME, DAMSON PLUMS HAVE ALWAYS CONJURED images of old-fashioned elegance, like something Anne of Green Gables would have helped Marilla put up during her young, orphaned years. I've learned that they are a marvelous, modern tasting little fruit, full of zip and pucker that create a most tasty and complicated jam. If you can't find them, ask one of the fruit growers at your local farmers' market: they just might have a stash that they'll be willing to share.

MAKES 4 (1-PINT/500 ML) JARS

8 cups damson plum pulp (from $4\frac{1}{2}$ pounds/
  2 kg plums, prepared as directed below; see note)
4 cups/800 g granulated sugar
Zest and juice of 1 lemon
2 (3-ounce/85 ml) packets liquid pectin

Prepare a boiling water bath and 4 regular-mouth 1-pint/500 ml jars according to the process on page 10. Place lids in a small saucepan, cover them with water, and simmer over very low heat

Combine the damson plum pulp with the sugar in a large, nonreactive pot and bring to a boil. Cook at a boil for 10 to 15 minutes, until the jam begins to look molten and syrupy. Add the lemon zest and juice and liquid pectin. Return to a boil and cook rapidly for 5 minutes.

Remove the pot from the heat and ladle the jam into the prepared jars. Wipe the rims, apply the lids and rings, and process in a boiling water bath for 10 minutes (see page 11).

Note: Because they are both tiny and firm fleshed, I've found that damson plums aren't fun to chop by hand. Instead, I recommend simmering them in 1 cup of water, until the skins pop and then pushing them through a colander, so that only the pits and a few wisps of skin are left behind.

AMY'S TOMATO JAM

SEVERAL SUMMERS AGO MY FRIEND AMY GAVE ME a jar of tomato jam with the recipe attached and now I can't go back to a life without it. I use it in place of ketchup, as well as in places where ketchup wouldn't dare to tread. (Try it with a soft, stinky cheese. It will change your life.) For those of you who are accustomed to preserving tomatoes, you'll notice that this recipe does not call for you to first peel them. This is not a mistake. The first time I made it, I thought I could improve on things and peeled and seeded the tomatoes prior to cooking them down. However, without those bits, the finished jam was too sweet and entirely without texture. It needs the skin and seeds to keep things interesting.

MAKES 4 (1-PINT/500 ML) JARS

5 pounds/2.3 kg tomatoes, cored and finely chopped
3 1/2 cups/700 g granulated sugar
1/2 cup/120 ml freshly squeezed lime juice
2 teaspoons grated peeled fresh ginger
1 teaspoon ground cinnamon
1/2 teaspoon ground cloves
1 tablespoon sea salt
1 tablespoon red pepper flakes

Combine all ingredients in a large, nonreactive pot. Bring to a boil over high heat and then reduce the heat to low. Simmer the jam, stirring regularly, until it reduces to a sticky, jammy mess. This will take between 1 1/2 and 2 hours.

When the jam is nearly done, prepare a boiling water bath and 4 regular-mouth 1-pint/500 ml jars according to the process on page 10. Place the lids in a small saucepan, cover them with water, and simmer over very low heat.

When the jam has cooked down sufficiently, remove the pot from the heat and ladle the jam into the prepared jars. Wipe the rims, apply the lids and rings, and process in a boiling water bath for 20 minutes (see page 11).

CHUNKY FIG JAM

THERE REALLY ISN'T MUCH THAT FIG JAM CAN'T DO. It goes incredibly well with an array of cheeses, from mild to stinky. It's a dream on roast pork. And don't even get me started on home-made Fig Newtons. It's no wonder that this is one of my favorite jams to have in the pantry. Depending on where you live, figs can get a little bit expensive. If they're beyond your budget, see if you can't find someone with a fig tree who would be willing to share their figs in exchange for a cut of the jam. It always seems like a fair trade to me!

MAKES 3 (1-PINT/500 ML) JARS

6 cups coarsely chopped fresh figs
  (about 3 pounds/1.4 kg whole figs)
4 cups/800 g granulated sugar
Juice of 2 lemons
1 (3-ounce/85 ml) packet liquid pectin

Prepare a boiling water bath and 3 regular-mouth 1-pint/500 ml jars according to the process on page 10. Place the lids in a small saucepan, cover them with water, and simmer over very low heat.

Combine the figs and sugar in a large pot and stir well to help the sugar pull the juice from the figs. When the mixture starts to look juicy, place the pot over high heat and bring to an active simmer. Cook for approximately 20 minutes, stirring regularly, until the figs have started to break down and the liquid starts to look syrupy.

Add the lemon juice and liquid pectin and return the figs to an active boil for 5 minutes.

Remove the pot from the heat and ladle the jam into the prepared jars. Wipe the rims, apply the lids and rings, and process in a boiling water bath for 10 minutes (see page 11).

fig jam

PEAR GINGER JAM

SEVERAL YEARS AGO, I STARTED SEEING THE PEAR-ginger combination everywhere. Companies were using it to flavor granolas and several different brands made a sweetened sparkling water drink with a pear-ginger flavor base. I liked the idea of those two tastes together and so took a stab at making something that featured them. This jam was the happy result. I've taught a number of early-winter canning classes using this recipe as the starting point and it never fails to make people swoon. It's really good heaped atop a stack of whole grain pancakes or swirled into oatmeal.

MAKES 4 (1-PINT/500 ML) JARS

**8 cups cored and chopped Bartlett or Anjou pears
(about 4 pounds/1.8 kg)**
4 cups/800 g granulated sugar
1 cup/240 ml ginger juice (see instructions on page 31)
2 (3-ounce/85 ml) packets liquid pectin

Prepare a boiling water bath and 4 regular-mouth 1-pint/500 ml jars according to the process on page 10. Place the lids in a small saucepan, cover them with water, and simmer over very low heat.

In a large, nonreactive pot, combine the chopped pears, sugar, and ginger juice. Cook over medium heat until the fruit can easily be smashed with the back of a wooden spoon. Use a potato masher or immersion blender to break the fruit down into a mostly smooth sauce.

Add the liquid pectin and bring to a rolling boil. Let boil for a full 5 minutes.

Remove the pot from the heat and ladle the jam into the prepared jars. Wipe the rims, apply the lids and rings, and process in a boiling water bath for 10 minutes (see page 11).

Note: As long as you choose a thin-skinned pear like a Bartlett or Anjou, there is no need to peel the pears for this recipe. I find that the skin just melts into the jam. However, with tougher skinned pears like Bosc, I would recommend peeling before cooking the fruit down into jam.

APPLE-CRANBERRY JAM

THIS IS A RECIPE I FIRST DEVISED AS A HOLIDAY gift. It produces a preserve that is festively crimson and works just as well with a slice of cold turkey as it does spread on toast. This recipe also has a larger yield than many others in this book. When you're canning for holiday giving, I've found that it's always handy to have a couple extra jars. No matter how well I plan, I always find that there's a neighbor or co-worker I've inadvertently left off the list.

MAKES 5 (1-PINT/500 ML) JARS

8 cups peeled, cored, and diced apples
   (about 4 pounds/1.8 kg apples; see note)
4 cups/400 g fresh cranberries
6 cups/1.2 kg granulated sugar
Zest and juice of 2 lemons

Prepare a boiling water bath and 5 regular-mouth 1-pint/500 ml jars according to the process on page 10. Place the lids in a small saucepan, cover them with water, and simmer over very low heat.

Combine the apples, cranberries, sugar, and 1 cup/240 ml water in a large pot (use a big one, as this jam will bubble). Bring to a boil over high heat, skimming off the foam that develops on the top of the fruit. Continue to boil for 15 to 20 minutes, until the cranberries pop and the apples soften.

Add the lemon zest and juice. Reduce the heat and simmer until the liquid in the pot has thickened, about 10 minutes. (Because both apples and cranberries are naturally high in pectin, you won't need any additional pectin to help this jam set, as long as you cook it until thick and syrupy).

Remove the pot from the heat and ladle the jam into the prepared jars. Wipe the rims, apply the lids and rings, and process in a boiling water bath for 10 minutes (see page 11).

Note: When choosing apples for jam or butter, it's good to pick a softer fleshed apple such as Golden Delicious, Cortland, or Winesap. I like to use a couple different varieties in each batch to increase the depth of flavor.

HONEY LEMON APPLE JAM

AFTER A BUSY SUMMER OF CANNING, I'M ALWAYS grateful when late fall arrives and the preserving frenzy cools down. By January, I start to itch for a reason to pull out the canning pot and fill a few jars. This recipe fills the bill and is actually the perfect thing for storage apples that have seen better days. They may not be so good for eating fresh, but they cook into applesauce and then jam like a dream.

MAKES 3 (1-PINT/500 ML) JARS

6 cups peeled, cored and chopped apples
  (about 3 pounds/1.4 kg apples; see note on page 47)
Zest and juice of 4 lemons
$2\frac{1}{2}$ cups/500 g granulated sugar
$\frac{1}{2}$ cup/120 ml honey

Prepare a boiling water bath and 3 regular-mouth 1-pint/500 ml jars according to the process on page 10. Place the lids in a small saucepan, cover them with water, and simmer over very low heat.

Combine the chopped apples and lemon juice in a large pot. Bring to the very barest of simmers over medium heat then reduce the heat to medium-low. Cook the apples down into a chunky sauce, stirring frequently, until they can easily be mashed with the back of a wooden spoon. This will take between 20 to 30 minutes, depending on the age of your apples. Once the apples are quite soft, smash them a bit more with a potato masher.

Add the sugar and honey. Increase the heat to medium-high and bring to a simmer. (At this point the jam will become quite splashy. Use a mesh splatter shield if you have one to keep the flying bits of jam off your arms and stovetop.)

After an additional 10 minutes of sputtering cooking, the jam should be thickening and quite sticky looking. Remove the pot from the heat and stir in the lemon zest. Ladle the jam into the prepared jars. Wipe the rims, apply the lids and rings, and process in a boiling water bath for 10 minutes (see page 11).

Clockwise from top: Nearly Seedless
Blackberry Sage Jam, Rhubarb Jam with
Strawberries and Oranges, Blueberry Jam,
Strawberry Vanilla Jam, Apple Cranberry Jam

FRUIT BUTTERS

MY FIRST INTRODUCTION TO FRUIT BUTTERS came through reading, not eating. During my early elementary school years, I was fascinated by those "When They Were Young" biographies about famous figures in history and read every one I could track down. It was in the book about fellow Philadelphian Betsy Ross that I discovered that butter could be something more than just the dairy product we spread on toast. The book described the young Betsy helping her mother by tending the huge pot of apple butter, as it slowly cooked down over an open fire. I wanted to do that, too.

A few years later, my family found ourselves living in a house in Portland, Oregon, that had a number of antique apple trees. Not wanting those apples to go to waste, my mom and I started making applesauce and later, apple butter. I got my wish.

These days, making fruit butters is a regular part of my year. I like them because they require less additional sweetener than jams and never need pectin. The trade-off you make when you cook up a batch of fruit butter is that your yield will always be smaller than with a batch of jam. But, as I am the only member of my household who likes these sweet spreads, this is actually a plus. Additionally, if you have a tree that produces a massive influx of fruit once a year, you'll also like this feature.

The other major difference between jams and fruit butters is that the butters get cooked low and slow for a good long time. I'm a big believer in using a slow cooker for fruit butters, because of its ability to produce low, even heat for extended periods of time. (Keep in mind that newer slow cookers cook hotter than the older ones. Because of this, the recipes that call for slow cookers offer a time range instead of a one-size-fits-all recommendation.)

You can also make fruit butters on the stovetop (when stove-topping it, I recommend one of those fine mesh splatter shields most commonly used for frying) or even in the oven. In the following recipes, I will elaborate on each of these techniques. However, you should know that just because a recipe calls for the stovetop method doesn't mean that you are wedded to the stovetop for that particular ingredient for all time. As you get more comfortable with the making of fruit butters, you'll find the method that appeals to you most.

There's one last thing to know about fruit butters. Because they have less sugar in them, they don't have the same shelf life as jams. Sugar is a powerful preservative, so if a product has less of it, it won't be able to hold off the ravages of time as well. This doesn't mean you shouldn't make fruit butters, it's just important to remember that they should be eaten within six to eight months of going into the jar.

ORANGE-RHUBARB BUTTER

THIS IS A PRESERVE FOR PEOPLE WHO LIKE THE marriage of sweet and tart. The orange plays with the rhubarb beautifully and the sugar serves as flavor brightener as much as sweetener. I particularly like it stirred into Greek yogurt and topped with toasted walnuts. Occasionally, I'll add a bit of ground cardamom to really good effect. Because this is a stovetop butter, it requires a bit more tending than ones made in the oven or slow cooker. It's great for those days when you've got multiple kitchen projects going, so that the regular stirring doesn't feel like a chore. If it starts to splash over your stove, top the pot with a splatter shield so that it can continue to cook down without making a mess.

MAKES 2 (1-PINT/500 ML) JARS

8 cups chopped rhubarb (about 3 pounds/1.4 kg rhubarb)
2 cups/400 g granulated sugar
2 cups/480 ml orange juice

Combine the rhubarb, sugar, and orange juice in a large, heavy saucepan and bring to a simmer. Reduce the heat to low and let it gently bubble, stirring every 5 minutes or so. If it's sticking to the bottom of the pot, lower the heat a bit more. Continue cooking like this for at least an hour, until the butter has reduced in volume and has turned a deep, rosy color.

Thirty minutes before the butter is finished, prepare a boiling water bath and 2 regular-mouth 1-pint/500 ml jars according to the process on page 10. Place the lids in a small saucepan, cover them with water, and simmer over very low heat.

When the butter is done, remove the pan from the heat and ladle the butter into the prepared jars. Wipe the rims, apply the lids and rings, and process in a boiling water bath for 15 minutes (see page 11).

The sealed jars can be stored in a cool, dry place for up to 6 months.

SWEET CHERRY BUTTER

CHERRY-FLAVORED FOODS OFTEN GET A BAD RAP. And really, artificial cherry syrups and candies deserve every ounce of the criticism they get. Happily, this fruit butter has absolutely nothing in common with those fakers. It is rich and complex, with more in common with really good wine than cough drops. It's important to acknowledge that pitting cherries is a lot of work. I recommend spending the money to buy a real pitter and committing to standing at the kitchen sink for the hour it will take. You'll be grateful come January.

MAKES 2 (1-PINT/500 ML) JARS

6 cups pitted and chopped sweet cherries
(about 3 pounds/1.4 kg cherries)
2 cups/400 g granulated sugar, divided
Juice of 1 lemon

Combine the cherries and 1½ cups/300 g of sugar in a large pot and bring to a simmer. Reduce the heat to low and let it gently bubble, stirring every 5 minutes or so. If it's sticking to the bottom, lower the heat a bit more. Cook like this for at least an hour, until the butter has reduced in volume and it has taken on a deep wine color.

Using an immersion blender (or working in batches in a blender), carefully purée the fruit. (I purée the butter after it has cooked down almost all the way because it splashes less during the cooking process this way.)

Taste and add the remaining sugar if you feel it needs it. Add the lemon juice and stir to combine. If it doesn't seem at all watery and the texture seems sufficiently thick, the butter is done. If not, continue to cook until the butter is thick and spreadable, keeping in mind that it will thicken a bit more as it cools.

When the butter is nearing completion, prepare a boiling water bath and 2 regular-mouth 1-pint/500 ml jars according to the process on page 10. Place the lids in a small saucepan, cover them with water, and simmer over very low heat.

When the butter is done, remove the pot from the heat and ladle it into the prepared jars. Wipe the rims, apply the lids and rings, and process in a boiling water bath for 15 minutes (see page 11).

The sealed jars can be stored in a cool, dry place for up to 6 months.

SLOW COOKER BLUEBERRY BUTTER

THOUGH I'VE BEEN A LIFELONG FAN OF BLUEBERRY
jam, it was only very recently that I took a stab at making blueberry
butter. The result is just wonderful: Less sweet and sticky than a
traditional jam, it ends up tasting like blueberry pie in a jar.

MAKES 3 (1-PINT/500 ML) JARS

8 cups puréed blueberries (about 3 dry quarts/1.7 kg blueberries)
2 cups/400 g granulated sugar
Zest and juice of 1 lemon
2 teaspoons ground cinnamon
½ teaspoon freshly grated nutmeg

Put the puréed blueberries in a 4-quart capacity slow cooker. Cover and turn it to low.
After it has cooked for 1 hour, remove the lid and stir. From this point forward, you will
want keep the lid slightly cracked. Propping it open with a wooden spoon or chopstick allows for the evaporating steam to escape.

This butter will need between 4 to 8 hours total in the slow cooker. The time varies
depending on how hot your slow cooker cooks. Check the butter at least once an
hour to track the progress.

In the final hour, add the sugar, lemon zest and juice, and spices. If you want to
speed the evaporation, remove the lid and turn the cooker up to high. If you do this,
make sure to check and stir the butter every 10 minutes to prevent scorching.

When the butter is nearing completion, Prepare a boiling water bath and 3 regular-
mouth 1-pint/500 ml jars according to the process on page 10. Place the lids in a
small saucepan, cover them with water, and simmer over very low heat.

Once it is as thick as ketchup and spreadable, determine whether you like a chunky
or smooth butter. Purée the butter for a smoother texture; for a slight chunkiness, leave
it as it is.

Turn the slow cooker off and ladle the butter into the prepared jars. Wipe the rims,
apply the lids and rings, and process in a boiling water bath for 10 minutes (see page 11).

The sealed jars can be stored in a cool, dry place for up to 6 months.

SLOW COOKER PEAR BUTTER ~

EACH FALL, I EAT THE SAME BREAKFAST EVERY morning for at least one month. It consists of a scoop of Greek yogurt, a tumble of granola, and a generous dollop of pear butter. Stirred together, it tastes like pear crisp topped with cream. With the help of the slow cooker, making pear butter couldn't be easier. The pears simply get cored and chopped (no need to peel) and cooked down in a slow cooker. Lightly sweetened and gently spiced, it's good for breakfast and even better as part of a cheese platter.

MAKE 3 (1-PINT/500 ML) JARS

10 cups cored and chopped pears (about 5 pounds/2.3 kg pears)
2 to 3 cups/400 to 600 g granulated sugar, or as needed
Zest and juice of 1 lemon
3 teaspoons ground cinnamon
1 teaspoon ground ginger
$\frac{1}{2}$ teaspoon freshly grated nutmeg

Place the pears in a 4-quart slow cooker. Cover and cook on low for 1 hour.

Remove the lid and give the pears a stir. From this point forward, you will want keep the lid slightly cracked. I have found that propping it open with a wooden spoon or chopstick gives just enough room for the evaporating steam to escape.

Continue to cook the pears down for an additional 5 to 7 hours, checking every hour and stirring. After it has cooked for 4 hours, blend the butter for a smoother texture. For a chunkier consistency, use a potato masher to help break down the pears.

In the final hour of cooking, taste the pears and add 2 to 3 cups of sugar. Use your judgment and taste buds to determine the correct sugar level. Add the lemon zest and juice and the spices and stir to combine.

If you need to speed up the process of cooking the pears down, remove the lid and turn the slow cooker to high. Stay close when it's on high and stir often.

When the butter is nearing completion, Prepare a boiling water bath and 3 regular-mouth 1-pint/500 ml jars according to the process on page 10. Place the lids in a small saucepan, cover them with water, and simmer over very low heat.

When it has reached a consistency that is thick and spreadable, ladle the butter into the prepared jars. Wipe the rims, apply the lids and rings, and process in a boiling water bath for 15 minutes (see page 11).

The sealed jars can be stored in a cool, dry place for up to 6 months.

APPLE PUMPKIN BUTTER

LOTS OF PEOPLE HAVE FOND MEMORIES OF EATING toast smeared with pumpkin butter. In recent days, food scientists have found that because of its density and low acidity, pumpkin butter isn't safe for home canning, even when using a pressure canner. That's why I recommend that you keep this butter in the freezer. Make sure not to skimp on the spices, as they help bring out the pumpkin flavor and create a truly autumnal butter.

MAKES 5 CUPS/1.5 KG

5 cups/1.21 kg Spiced Applesauce (page 190)
3 cups/750 g plain pumpkin purée (canned is perfectly fine)
3 cups/600 g granulated sugar
Juice of 1 lemon
2 tablespoons ground cinnamon
1 teaspoon freshly grated nutmeg
1 teaspoon ground ginger

Combine the applesauce and pumpkin purée in a large pot. Bring to a gentle simmer and then reduce the heat to low. Cook over low heat for at least 1 hour, stirring every 10 minutes to prevent sticking. If the butter begins to spurt out of the pot, use a splatter shield to keep things neat.

After the first hour of cooking, stir the sugar, lemon juice, and spices into the butter. Stir and continue to cook over low heat, until the butter is thick and spreadable, about 30 to 45 minutes.

Remove the pot from the heat and ladle the butter into freezer-safe jars. The butter can be kept in the freezer for up to 1 year.

OVEN-ROASTED PEACH BUTTER

THERE ARE SOME WHO SAY THAT IT'S IMPOSSIBLE to improve on a fresh summer peach. To them I say, try this peach butter. The oven roasting concentrates the flavor of the peaches and transforms them into a rich, spreadable condiment that is glorious on top of whole-wheat biscuits or just eaten straight with a spoon. This butter is easily made in larger batches with increased quantities.

MAKES 3 (HALF-PINT/250 ML) JARS

3 pounds/1.4 kg yellow peaches
1 to 2 cups/200 to 400 g granulated sugar, or as needed
Zest and juice of 1 lemon

Preheat the oven to 350°F/180°C/gas 4. Prepare a boiling water bath and 3 regular-mouth half-pint/250 ml jars according to the process on page 10. Place the lids in a small saucepan, cover them with water, and simmer over very low heat.

Cut the peaches in half and remove the pits. Arrange them cut-side down in a single layer in a nonreactive baking dish (glass or ceramic is best). Roast for 30 minutes, or until the skins are loose.

Remove the baking dish from the oven and remove the skins from the peach halves and discard. Using a fork, mash the softened peaches in the baking dish. Reduce the oven temperature to 250°F/120°C/gas ½. Return the mashed peaches to the oven and bake for an additional 2 to 3 hours, checking often to stir and prevent burning, until all the wateriness is gone and they are dark in color.

When the peaches have broken down sufficiently, taste the fruit and stir in 1 cup/200g sugar. Taste and add more sugar to taste. Stir in the lemon zest and juice.

Because this recipe makes such a small amount, I tend to skip the boiling water bath step and just keep it in the refrigerator. If you are short on fridge space, this butter can be processed for 15 minutes in a boiling water bath (see page 11).

JELLIES

WHEN I FIRST STARTED CANNING, I DIDN'T really get jelly. I didn't understand why anyone would mess around with something that was so seemingly fussy when there was a whole world of jams and fruit butters. But then someone presented me with a jar of homemade quince jelly and I got it. It wasn't fussy, it was refined. Making jelly is all about the extraction and concentration of flavors and it is worth the energy it takes to create a jar of wiggly, translucent fruit flavor.

That said, I'll be the first to tell you that I'm something of a cheater. Three of the jellies in this section start with pre-pressed or -squeezed juice. This is a choice that will make some purists grimace. I have found that as long as you start with high-quality juice, you can make a very good jelly and save yourself a whole lot of work.

As you head into jelly making, know that your first batch might not turn out perfectly. Jelly is a fickle preserve that can be affected by altitude, humidity, and the ratios of sugar to water in the juice you're working with. Keep trying and don't get discouraged.

To give your jelly the best chance for success, there are a few things you can do. Make sure to stash several small plates or saucers in the freezer at least an hour before you start cooking so that you can test your jelly as it cooks. Keep your thermometer close at hand. And make sure to keep a clear space next to the stove in case you need to move the pot off the burner quickly if it threatens to boil over.

You will note that there are a few recipes in this section that call for powdered pectin in place of liquid pectin. Powdered pectin sets up more firmly than liquid, which is a boon when you're trying to transform fruit juice into jelly. Make sure to whisk it fully into the sugar before beginning cooking, so that the pectin will be evenly distributed in the juice and won't clump up during cooking.

MIMOSA JELLY

THIS JELLY STRIVES TO BE A SPREADABLE VERSION of that beloved weekend brunch cocktail. It combines the tang of freshly squeezed orange juice with the pleasant buzz of sparkling wine. If you're looking for a good party favor for a bridal shower, put this jelly up in those adorable, 4-ounce/120 ml jelly jars and tie on a tag with a length of striped bakery twine. The cuteness of it all is certain to make your guests swoon.

MAKES 3 (1-PINT/500 ML) JARS

4 cups/960 ml freshly squeezed orange juice
1 cup/240 ml sparkling wine
4 cups/800 g granulated sugar
2 (3-ounce/85 ml) packets liquid pectin

Prepare a boiling water bath and 3 regular-mouth 1-pint/500 ml jars according to the process on page 10. Place the lids in a small saucepan, cover them with water, and simmer over very low heat.

In a large, nonreactive pot, combine the orange juice, sparkling wine, and sugar and bring them to a boil over high heat heat. Cook, stirring frequently, for 15-25 minutes, until the volume in the pot is greatly reduced. While you continue to stir, clip a candy thermometer to the pot and watch until the jelly reaches 220°F/105°C. It should look thick and syrupy and the bubbles should look like bright orange molten lava.

Add the liquid pectin and boil for an additional 5 minutes. Test the set of the jelly using the saucer test described on page 77. If it doesn't pass, return the pot to the heat and cook for an additional 5 minutes before repeating the test.

When the jelly has reached the desired consistency, pour it into the prepared jars. Wipe the rims, apply the lids and rings, and process in a boiling water bath for 10 minutes (see page 11).

QUINCE JELLY ～↗〜

QUINCE IS SOMEWHAT OBSCURE BUT ABSOLUTELY worth tracking down. It has fuzzy skin like a peach and smells intensely floral when fresh. It has incredibly dense flesh and is far too astringent to be eaten raw. When the flesh is chopped and simmered with water, it relaxes, turns vividly red and becomes wonderfully edible. It is the primary ingredient in membrillo, that rosy-hued fruit paste that is often served with Spanish cheese. Look for it in your local farmers' markets or ask an area orchard if they have some you can buy.

MAKES 4 (HALF-PINT/250 ML) JARS

5 pounds/2.3 kg quince
4 cups/800 grams granulated sugar
1/3 cup freshly squeezed lemon juice

Core the quince and chop it into rough cubes. Combine quince pieces with 3 quarts/2.8 liters of water in a large stock pot set over high heat. Bring the water to a boil, reduce the heat to medium, and simmer for 2 to 3 hours, until the fruit and liquid turn a deep pink color. The liquid should have reduced by approximately half and the chunks of quince should be very soft when crushed with the back of a wooden spoon. When it's done, strain the juice from the pulp using a fine mesh sieve or jelly bag, taking care not to pressure or squeeze the quince pulp. Forcing liquid from the pulp will make your jelly cloudy. Let pulp drain for 3 to 4 hours, reserving the juice.

Prepare a boiling water bath and 4 half-pint/250 ml jars according to the process on page 10. Place the lids in a small saucepan, cover them with water, and simmer over very low heat.

In a large, nonreactive pot, combine 5 cups/1.2 liters of the reserved quince juice, sugar, and lemon juice and bring them to a boil over high heat. Cook, stirring frequently, for 15 to 25 minutes, until the volume in the pot is greatly reduced. Clip a candy thermometer to the pot and stir occasionally until the jelly reaches 220°F/105°C. It should look thick, with the bubbles like molten lava.

When the jelly has reached 220°F/105°C, pour it into the prepared jars. Wipe the rims, apply the lids and rings, and process in a boiling water bath for 10 minutes (see page 11).

RHUBARB JELLY

SINCE MOVING TO THE EAST COAST, RHUBARB HAS become my personal indicator that spring is finally on the way. When it arrives, I buy it by the armload and make butters, jams, compotes, and this ruby-colored jelly. It tastes tart and clean, just as a new season should.

MAKES 4 (HALF-PINT/250 ML) JARS

1 ½ pounds/680 g rhubarb, chopped
3 cups/600 g granulated sugar
1 (1.75 ounce/50 g) packet powdered pectin

Combine the chopped rhubarb and 3 cups/720 ml water in a pot. Cover and simmer for 20 to 25 minutes, or until the rhubarb has completely broken down and the water is tinted a vivid pink.

Line a large, fine-mesh sieve with cheesecloth and place it over a large bowl. Pour the cooked rhubarb through. Let it sit and drip for at least 30 minutes. Do not press the rhubarb pulp, as that will make your jelly cloudy. Discard the solids in the sieve and measure out 4 cups/960 ml of rhubarb juice.

Prepare a boiling water bath and 4 half-pint/250 ml jars according to the process on page 10. Place the lids in a small saucepan, cover them with water, and simmer over very low heat.

Measure the sugar into a bowl. Whisk the powdered pectin into the sugar to blend.

In a large, nonreactive pot, combine the rhubarb juice and the pectin-spiked sugar.

Bring to a boil and cook over high heat for 15 to 25 minutes, stirring frequently, until the volume in the pot is greatly reduced. While you continue to stir, clip a candy thermometer to the pot and watch until the pot reaches 220°F/105°C. There will be a great deal of foaming and bubbling before it reaches this point. It should look thick and syrupy and the bubbles should look glossy.

Test the set of the jelly using the saucer test described on page 77. If it doesn't pass, return the pot to the heat and cook for an additional 5 minutes before repeating the test.

When the jelly has reached the desired consistency, pour it into the prepared jars. Wipe the rims, apply the lids and rings, and process in a boiling water bath for 10 minutes (see page 11).

MULLED CIDER JELLY

THIS JELLY TASTES LIKE A SPREADABLE VERSION of autumn. It reminds me of pumpkin patches, the night before Thanksgiving, and the pomander balls we used to make as kids, all spice and fragrance. After you use it on peanut butter sandwiches and morning toast, try it melted down and brushed on roast chicken or tofu.

MAKES 4 (HALF-PINT/250 ML) JARS

3 cups/600 g granulated sugar

1 (1.75 ounce/50 g packet) powdered pectin

4 cups/960 ml fresh pressed apple cider

Zest of 1 orange

2 teaspoons ground cinnamon

1 teaspoon ground ginger

$\frac{1}{2}$ teaspoon freshly grated nutmeg

$\frac{1}{2}$ teaspoon ground cloves

Prepare a boiling water bath and 4 half-pint/250 ml jars according to the process on page 10. Place the lids in a small saucepan, cover them with water, and simmer over very low heat.

Measure the sugar into a bowl. Whisk the powdered pectin into the sugar to blend.

In a large, nonreactive pot, combine the apple cider and the pectin-spiked sugar. Add the orange zest and spices. Bring to a boil and cook over high heat for 15-25 minutes, stirring frequently, until the volume in the pot is greatly reduced. While you continue to stir, clip a candy thermometer to the pot and watch until the pot reaches 220°F/105°C. There will be a great deal of foaming and bubbling before it reaches this point. It should look thick and syrupy and the bubbles should look glossy.

Test the set of the jelly using the saucer test described on page 77. If it doesn't pass, return the pot to the heat and cook for an additional 5 minutes before repeating the test. When the jelly has reached the desired consistency, pour it into the prepared jars. Wipe the rims, apply the lids and rings, and process in a boiling water bath for 10 minutes (see page 11).

CONCORD GRAPE JELLY

Y MEMORIES OF GRAPE JELLY ARE INEXTRICABLY linked to my childhood. Though we were more of a strawberry jam kind of family, my maternal grandparents regularly stocked Smucker's Concord Grape Jelly in their refrigerator. When we visited, I would beg to be allowed a slice of white bread toast, smeared with margarine and this grape jelly. While I opt for real butter and whole grain bread these days, I still love the flavor of Concord jelly on a slice of toast.

MAKES 4 (HALF-PINT/250 ML) JARS

3 cups/600 g granulated sugar
1 (1.75 ounce/50 g packet) powdered pectin
4 cups/960 ml unsweetened Concord grape juice

Prepare a boiling water bath and 4 half-pint/250 ml jars according to the process on page 10. Place the lids in a small saucepan, cover them with water, and simmer over very low heat.

Measure the sugar into a bowl. Whisk the powdered pectin into the sugar to blend.

In a large, nonreactive pot, combine the grape juice and the pectin-spiked sugar.

Bring to a boil and cook over high heat for 15 to 25 minutes, stirring frequently, until the volume in the pot is greatly reduced. While you continue to stir, clip a candy thermometer to the pot and watch until the pot reaches 220°F/105°C. There will be a great deal of foaming and bubbling before it reaches this point. It should look thick and syrupy and the bubbles should look glossy.

Test the set of the jelly using the saucer test described on page 77. If it doesn't pass, return the pot to the heat and cook for an additional 5 minutes before repeating the test. When the jelly has reached the desired consistency, pour it into the prepared jars. Wipe the rims, apply the lids and rings, and process in a boiling water bath for 10 minutes (see page 11).

MEYER LEMON JELLY

EACH YEAR DURING MEYER LEMON SEASON, I ORDER at least ten pounds from an organic orchard in California. I make Meyer Lemon Curd (page 89), Meyer Lemon Marmalade (page 79), and at least one batch of this jelly. It concentrates their bright flavor and is wonderful in cocktails, vinaigrettes, and for smearing on crêpes. Because Meyer lemons are so high in pectin, this recipe does not call for commercial pectin. However, don't skip the step that has you bundling the seeds into cheesecloth and simmering them with the jelly. They lend the bulk of the pectin to the mixture and help it transform from syrup to something more solid and spreadable.

MAKES 3 (HALF-PINT/250 ML) JARS

2½ cups/600 ml freshly squeezed Meyer lemon juice,
   seeds reserved (from about 20 lemons)
2 cups/400 g granulated sugar

Prepare a boiling water bath and 3 half-pint/250 ml jars according to the process on page 10. Place the lids in a small saucepan, cover them with water, and simmer over very low heat.

Place the reserved seeds in the center of a 6-inch/15 cm length of cheesecloth. Roll the cheesecloth up and tie it tightly so that no seeds are able to escape.

In a large, nonreactive pot, combine Meyer lemon juice, sugar, and the bundle of seeds.

Bring to a boil and cook over high heat for 15 to 25 minutes, stirring frequently, until the volume in the pot is greatly reduced. While you continue to stir, clip a candy thermometer to the pot and watch until it reaches 220°F/105°C. It should look thick and syrupy and the bubbles should look glossy.

Test the set of the jelly using the saucer test described on page 77. If it doesn't pass, return the pot to the heat and cook for an additional 5 minutes before repeating the test.

When the jelly has reached the desired consistency, pour it into the prepared jars. Wipe the rims, apply the lids and rings, and process in a boiling water bath for 10 minutes (see page 11).

MARMALADES

DURING MY CHILDHOOD, I WAS NEVER MUCH FOR marmalade. When it came to peanut butter sandwiches, my sister and I preferred the strawberry jam that came in a blue plastic tub with a white lid and handle, like a little bucket. My mom always had a stash of something homemade tucked in the back of the fridge for her toast, while my dad typically gravitated towards the squeeze bottle of honey.

The only person I knew who kept marmalade on his grocery list was my grandpa Sid. He preferred Smucker's and liked a fine layer on a piece of morning toast. On occasion, he'd offer me a bite, and I always found it displeasingly bitter and not nearly sweet enough for my young taste buds.

It wasn't until several years ago, while watching the movie *Gosford Park*, that I reconsidered marmalade. There's one scene, in the final third of the movie, in which Maggie Smith's character is having breakfast in her room with her lady's maid. She lifts a cut-glass lid from a preserves jar and complains bitterly when she discovers that the marmalade it contains was store-bought, as opposed to being homemade. That scene settled into the depths of my brain and took root, sending out shoots that said "homemade marmalade is always preferable to mass-produced."

Eventually, I gave it a shot. My first attempts were crude, though not entirely unappealing. I liked it enough to keep trying. In the years since, I have made marmalade every late winter, counting on it as talisman against the January blues.

Because marmalade uses the entirety of the fruit, I like to make sure I use the best I can find. Choose backyard or organic fruit, and wash it well in warm, soapy water. Living in Philadelphia means that backyard fruit is a fantasy for me, but during the citrus season, I'll often invest in a box of handpicked, pesticide-free fruit from Texas, Florida, or California. Local Harvest (localharvest.com) is a really good resource for tracking down reliable, well-regarded citrus growers.

Marmalade making requires a few additional pieces of equipment that are rarely used in other fruit preserves. Before you get started, make sure you have a length of cheesecloth handy in which to bundle up the seeds and other pectin-rich bits of fruit. You can also use a large, stainless steel tea ball. Additionally, since these spreads are almost entirely made without the aid of commercial pectin, you'll need a good thermometer to track the temperature of the cooking marmalade. I like to use an old-fashioned candy thermometer. I used to have a fancy digital one, but the probe stopped working after I dropped the whole thing into a pot of boiling marmalade. The analog ones are far more resilient.

In addition to tracking the temperature, I also believe in using the saucer test when making marmalades. At the beginning of cooking, place two or three small saucers or plates in the freezer to chill. When your marmalade is at the end of its cooking time, dollop a small spoonful of jam onto the center of the frozen plate and return it to the freezer for one to two minutes. The goal is to speed up its natural cooling process and see what the finished set will be like.

The hope is that it will firm up quickly and form a "skin" across the top of the puddle that will wrinkle when gently nudged with a fingertip. That means it's done. However, if the jam doesn't wrinkle and maintains a more syrupy consistency after a few minutes on the cold plate, it needs more cooking.

Several of these recipes call for powdered pectin. I prefer it to liquid pectin when making marmalades and jellies, as it has the ability to set more firmly. That's not always a consistency you want with jam, but it's highly desirable with marmalades.

THREE CITRUS MARMALADE ⁓

THIS IS A LOVELY JAM FOR CITRUS LOVERS. IT doesn't force you to play favorites and shows off all those bright, punchy citrus flavors. In addition to its many normal applications, I like to use a couple of dollops while quickly sautéeing sliced chicken breast. Served over steamed brown rice and with a side of broccoli, it's my cheap (and healthier) version of Chinese orange chicken take-out.

MAKES 4 (1-PINT/500 ML) JARS

4 pounds/1.8 kg assorted citrus fruit
  (I like to use 3 pink grapefruit, 4 lemons, and 5 navel oranges)
6 cups/1.2 kg granulated sugar

Wash the fruit in warm, soapy water and dry thoroughly. Using a serrated-edge vegetable peeler, remove the zest from the fruit. Stack the zest strips in piles and chop into fine confetti. Combine the zest in a pot with 2 quarts/2 liters filtered water. Bring to a boil, reduce the heat to medium-high, and simmer for 25 to 30 minutes, until zest ribbons are tender.

While the zest cooks, "supreme" the fruit by cutting the white pith away from the fruit and cutting the fruit into segments between the membranes. Collect the fruit and any juices in a large bowl and remove the seeds as you go, setting them aside.

When all the fruit has been segmented out, bundle the seeds into a length of cheesecloth, tying the ends of the cloth securely so that no seeds can escape.

Drain the zest in a fine-mesh sieve, reserving the cooking liquid.

Prepare a boiling water bath and 4 regular-mouth 1-pint/500 ml jars according to the process on page 10. Place the lids in a small saucepan, cover them with water, and simmer over very low heat.

In a pot, combine the drained zest, segmented citrus fruit and juice, 4 cups/960 ml of the reserved cooking liquid, the sugar, and the cheesecloth bundle. Bring to a vigorous boil and cook until the mixture reaches 220°F/105°C (this takes between 30 and 40 minutes). Stir regularly as it cooks to prevent scorching.

When the marmalade reaches 220°F/105°C and sustains that temperature for 1 minute (even after stirring), remove the pot from the heat. Test the set of the marmalade using the saucer test described on page 77. If it doesn't pass, return the pot to the heat and cook for an additional 5 minutes before repeating the test. Once it seems to be setting to your satisfaction, remove the pot from the heat and remove the cheesecloth bundle. Stir marmalade for about 1 minute, to help the zest bits become evenly distributed throughout the preserves.

Ladle the marmalade into the prepared jars. Wipe the rims, apply the lids and rings, and process in a boiling water bath for 10 minutes (see page 11).

MEYER LEMON MARMALADE

WHEN I WAS YOUNG, MY GRANDMA BUNNY LIVED in an asymmetrical ranch house in Woodland Hills, California. It was perched on a hillside and the air around the house smelled like eucalyptus leaves, rosemary, and Meyer lemons. She was the proudest Meyer lemon mama you'd ever meet and enjoyed evangelizing their many virtues. Though I can't prove it, I think she may have been behind their renewed popularity. I'm certain Bunny would have loved this marmalade, because it manages to both capture and enhance the flavor of these bracing, thin-skinned orange-lemon hybrids. Because I can't bear to waste even a smidgen of a good Meyer, this is a marmalade recipe that uses the whole fruit. Because of this, it does need an overnight rest in the fridge before using, to help break down the white pith and render it a bit less bitter.

MAKES 4 (1-PINT/500 ML) JARS

3 pounds/1.4 kg Meyer lemons (approximately 20 lemons)
5$\frac{1}{2}$ cups/1.1 kg granulated sugar, divided

Wash the lemons in warm, soapy water and dry thoroughly. Using a very sharp knife, cut both the flower and stem ends off the fruit. Sit each trimmed lemon on one of its newly flat ends and cut it into 6 wedges. Lay each wedge on its side and cut away the strip of inner membrane and the seeds. Reserve the trimmed pith and seeds (we'll be using them as a pectin source).

Take each trimmed wedge (it should look a bit like a pyramid with its top cut off), lay it rind-side up, and thinly slice from one pointy tip to the other. What you want to end up with are bits of lemon that are no more than a $\frac{1}{4}$-inch/6 mm thick ($\frac{1}{8}$-inch/3 mm thick is even better) and no more than $1\frac{1}{4}$ inches/4 cm in length. Repeat this with all the lemons.

Combine the lemon slices in a bowl or container that will fit in your fridge (I like to use a $\frac{1}{2}$ gallon/2 liter canning jar) and add 2 cups/400 g sugar. Stir to help the sugar dissolve. Bundle up the reserved seeds into a length of cheesecloth, tie the ends tightly and pop that into the container as well. Place it in the refrigerator overnight (it can be left this way up to 48 hours, which is good for those of us who lead busy lives).

Prepare a boiling water bath and 4 regular-mouth 1-pint/500 ml jars according to the process on page 10. Place the lids in a small saucepan, cover them with water, and simmer over very low heat.

After an overnight rest, pour the macerated lemon bits with their juice and the seed bundle into a pot. Add the remaining $3\frac{1}{2}$ cups/700 g sugar and 6 cups/1.4 liter water. Slowly bring to a boil over high heat, stirring regularly. Once it has reached a boil, attach the candy thermometer to the pot.

Continue to cook vigorously until the mixture reaches 220°F/105°C (this takes between 30 and 40 minutes). Stir regularly as it cooks to prevent scorching.

When the marmalade reaches 220°F/105°C and sustains that temperature for 1 minute (even after stirring), remove the pot from the heat. Test the set of the marmalade using the saucer test described on page 77. If it doesn't pass, return the pot to the heat and cook for an additional 5 minutes before repeating the test. Once it seems to be setting to your satisfaction, remove the pot from the heat and stir for about 1 minute, to help the zest bits become evenly distributed throughout the preserves.

Ladle the marmalade into the prepared jars. Wipe the rims, apply the lids and rings, and process in a boiling water bath for 10 minutes (see page 11).

CARA CARA ORANGE- GINGER MARMALADE

FROM THE OUTSIDE, CARA CARA ORANGES LOOK like any other orange. However, when you slice into them, the flesh is a brilliant pink and they smell ever so slightly of cranberries. Combined with ginger juice, they make a gorgeous marmalade that has just a touch of gingery sharpness upon the initial taste.

MAKES 7 (HALF-PINT/250 ML) JARS

4 pounds/1.8 kg Cara Cara oranges (about 8 or 9)

6 cups/1.2 kg granulated sugar

2 teaspoons powdered pectin (optional; see note)

1 cup/240 ml ginger juice (see page 31)

¼ cup/60 ml freshly squeezed lemon juice

Wash the fruit in warm, soapy water and dry thoroughly. Using a serrated-edge vegetable peeler, remove the zest from the fruit. Stack the zest strips in piles and chop into fine confetti. Combine the zest in a pot with 2 quarts/2 liters water. Bring to a boil, reduce the heat to medium-high, and simmer for 25 to 30 minutes, until zest ribbons are tender.

While the zest cooks, "supreme" the fruit by cutting the white pith away from the fruit and cutting the fruit into segments between the membranes. Collect the fruit and any juices in a large measuring cup.

Drain the zest in a fine-mesh sieve, reserving the cooking liquid.

Prepare a boiling water bath, 3 regular-mouth 1-pint/500 ml jars, and 1 half-pint/250 ml jar according to the process on page 10. Place the lids in a small saucepan, cover them with water, and simmer over very low heat.

In a large pot, combine the drained zest, segmented fruit, 4 cups/960 ml of the reserved cooking liquid, the sugar (if you're using the powdered pectin, whisk it into the sugar before adding it to the fruit), and 1 cup/240 ml ginger juice.

Bring to a boil and cook vigorously until the mixture reaches 220°F/105°C (this takes between 30 and 40 minutes). Stir regularly as it cooks to prevent scorching.

(continued)

When the marmalade reaches 220°F/105°C and sustains that temperature for 1 minute (even after stirring), remove the pot from the heat. Test the set of the marmalade using the saucer test described on page 77. If it doesn't pass, return the pot to the heat and cook for an additional 5 minutes before repeating the test. Once it seems to be setting to your satisfaction, remove the pot from the heat and stir for 1 minute, to help the zest bits become evenly distributed throughout the preserve.

Ladle the marmalade into the prepared jars. Wipe the rims, apply the lids and rings, and process in a boiling water bath for 10 minutes (see page 11).

Note: I call for an optional 2 teaspoons of pectin in this recipe. Typically you don't need to include it in marmalade because the seeds contain so much pectin. However, Cara Cara oranges are a nearly seedless hybrid, so we can't depend on them for a pectin boost. You can achieve a loose set just by cooking this marmalade to 220°F/105°C. For a firmer marmalade, additional pectin is required.

HONEY LEMON MARMALADE

'VE LEARNED THAT EVERY JANUARY, I COME DOWN with a miserable cold that is best treated with a day on the couch and many steaming mugs of honey, ginger, and lemon tea. This marmalade evokes those infusions, and makes me want to stir a spoonful into a glass of hot water. Because the honey plays such a dominant role, make sure to choose one that tastes good to you. I particularly like buckwheat honey for its assertive grassiness. Blackberry or wildflower honeys are also good choices. Note the overnight sitting time and plan accordingly.

MAKES 4 (1-PINT/500 ML) JARS

4½ pounds/2 kg lemons
4 cups/800 g sugar
2 cups/480 ml honey

Wash the fruit in warm, soapy water and dry thoroughly. Using a very sharp knife, cut both the flower and stem ends off the fruit. Set each trimmed lemon on one of its newly flat ends and cut it into 6 wedges. Lay each wedge on its side and cut away the strip of inner membrane and seeds. Reserve the seeds (we'll be using them as a pectin source).

Take a trimmed wedge (it should look a bit like a pyramid with its top cut off), lay it rind-side up and thinly slice from one point to the other. What you want to end up with are bits of lemon that are no more than a $1/4$-inch/6 mm thick ($1/8$-inch/3 mm thick is even better) and no more than 1 to $1 1/2$ inches/2.5 to 4 cm in length. Repeat this with all the lemons.

Bundle up the reserved seeds in a length of cheesecloth and tie the ends well, so that no seeds can escape.

Heap the lemon slices into a nonreactive pot with the seed bundle and add 2 quarts/2 liters water. Bring to a boil over high heat. As soon as the fruit has reached a rolling boil, remove the pot from the heat. Cover the pot and let it sit at room temperature overnight.

On day two, prepare a boiling water bath and 4 regular-mouth 1-pint/500 ml jars according to the process on page 10. Place the lids in a small saucepan, cover them with water, and simmer over very low heat.

Remove the seed bundle from the pot and discard. Strain the fruit, reserving all the liquid. Put the softened lemon into your jam pot. Measure out 6 cups/1.4 liters of the cooking liquid and pour it into the pot. Add the sugar and honey and bring to a boil. Cook vigorously over high heat until the mixture reaches 220°F/105°C (this takes between 30 and 40 minutes). Stir regularly as it cooks to prevent scorching.

When the marmalade reaches 220°F/105°C and sustains that temperature for 1 minute (even after stirring), remove the pot from the heat. Test the set of the marmalade using the saucer test described on page 77. If it doesn't pass, return the pot to the heat and cook for an additional 5 minutes before repeating the test. Once it seems to be setting to your satisfaction, remove the pot from the heat and stir for about 1 minute, to help the zest bits become evenly distributed throughout the preserve.

Ladle the marmalade into the prepared jars. Wipe the rims, apply the lids and rings, and process in a boiling water bath for 10 minutes (see page 11).

BLOOD ORANGE MARMALADE

WHEN BLOOD ORANGES WERE FIRST INTRODUCED to the American market in the 1930s, marketers tried to brand them "citrus tomatoes," fearing that shoppers would be put off by thoughts of bodily fluid. Thankfully, the name never caught on. These scarlet-fleshed fruits drip with crimson juice and make the most wonderfully hued marmalade.

MAKES 3 (1-PINT/500 ML) JARS

3½ pounds/1.6 kg blood oranges (about 10 to 12)
6 cups/1.2 kg sugar
2 teaspoons powdered pectin (optional; see note on page 82)

Wash the fruit in warm, soapy water and dry thoroughly. Using a serrated-edge vegetable peeler, remove the zest from the fruit. Stack the zest strips in piles and chop into fine confetti. Combine the zest in a pot with 2 quarts/2 liters water. Bring to a boil, reduce the heat to medium-high, and simmer for 25 to 30 minutes, until zest ribbons are tender.

While the zest cooks, "supreme" the fruit by cutting the white pith away from the fruit and cutting the fruit into segments between the membranes. Collect the fruit and any juices in a large measuring cup.

Drain the zest in a fine-mesh sieve, reserving the cooking liquid.

Prepare a boiling water bath and 3 regular-mouth 1-pint/500 ml jars according to the process on page 10. Place the lids in a small saucepan, cover them with water, and simmer over very low heat.

In a large pot, combine the drained zest, the segmented fruit and any juices, 6 cups/1.4 liters of the reserved cooking liquid, and the sugar (if you are using the powdered pectin, whisk it into the sugar before adding it to the fruit).

Bring to a boil and cook vigorously over high heat until the mixture reaches 220°F/105°C (this takes between 30 and 40 minutes). Stir regularly as it cooks to prevent scorching.

When the marmalade reaches 220°F/105°C and sustains that temperature for 1 minute (even after stirring), remove the pot from the heat. Test the set of the marmalade using the saucer test described on page 77. If it doesn't pass, return the pot to the heat and cook for an additional 5 minutes before repeating the test. Once it seems to be setting to your satisfaction, remove the pot from the heat and stir for about 1 minute, to help the zest bits become evenly distributed throughout the preserve.

Ladle the marmalade into the prepared jars. Wipe the rims, apply the lids and rings, and process in a boiling water bath for 10 minutes (see page 11).

Blood Orange Marmalade, Meyer Lemon Marmalade

CURDS & CONSERVES

OST PEOPLE THINK THAT CITRUS CURDS BELONG
to the world of high teas and clotted cream. However, if you've
never tasted freshly cooked curd, you're missing out on one of
the more delicious moments in life. It has an impossibly smooth texture that
is set off by the pucker of the citrus.

When you make a batch of citrus curd, make sure that you use the best eggs
and butter you can afford. I like to search out free-range eggs that have naturally bright orange yolks, as their color will help to enhance the vivid hue of the
finished curd. It should be as sunny as possible.

You'll notice that these curd recipes makes just a single pint (500 ml).
Because this isn't a preserve that needs to boil for an extended period to
reduce, as long as you have a large enough double boiler, you can double and
even triple the recipe. However, do note that when canning this one, it is recommended that you opt for either 4- or 8-ounce (125 or 250 ml) jars. The
smaller jars allow the heat to penetrate fully throughout the jars during processing and ensure a safer final product. What's more, you shouldn't make
more than you can eat or give away in the span of a couple months; these have
a shelf life of no more than 3 to 4 months.

Conserves are on the other side of the preserve spectrum from curds. They
are jams that have been enriched by the addition of dried fruit, nuts, coconut,
or liquors. They tend to be a bit less sweet than your average jam and have a
more varied texture, thanks to the addition of the bits of nuts or dried fruit
spread throughout.

I find that conserves make excellent gifts, because they are different from
the standard preserves that are easily bought at grocery stores and gourmet
markets.

MEYER LEMON CURD

THE FIRST TIME I TASTED LEMON CURD, I FELL HARD.
I was eleven years old and my family had received a jar of homemade lemon curd from some California cousins. They kept chickens
in their backyard with lemon trees out front, and so made jars of curd
using these homegrown ingredients to send to friends and family for the
holidays. I ate the bulk of that jar in stealthy spoonfuls.

MAKES 2 (HALF-PINT/250 ML) JARS

$^{1}/_{4}$ cup/80 g finely grated Meyer lemon zest
  (about 4 medium Meyer lemons)
$1^{1}/_{4}$ cups/250 g granulated sugar
4 large egg yolks
2 large eggs
$^{1}/_{2}$ cup/120 ml Meyer lemon juice
6 tablespoons/85 g cold unsalted butter, cut into cubes

Prepare a boiling water bath and 2 half-pint/250 ml jars according to the process on
page 10. Place the lids in a small saucepan, cover them with water, and simmer over
very low heat.

Combine the lemon zest and sugar in a small bowl. Rub the zest into the sugar until
it is fragrant and fully combined. Set aside.

Set up a double boiler, add 2 inches/5 cm of water to the bottom pan and bring to
a simmer over medium heat. Alternatively, set a heatproof mixing bowl over a
medium saucepan filled with 2 inches/5 cm of water, making sure the bottom of the
bowl does not touch the surface of the water. Keeping the top half of the double boiler
off the stove, combine the egg yolks and whole eggs and whisk them together. Add
the zest and sugar combination and whisk in. Finally, add the lemon juice and stir until
it is blended.

Add the butter and set the top of the double boiler over the simmering water.
Switch to a silicone spatula and stir continually as the lemon curd cooks.

Using a candy thermometer, monitor the temperature of the curd while you stir. As
it approaches 190° to 200°F/90° to 95°C, it should start to thicken. One sign of
(continued)

doneness is that it will coat the back of your spatula without running or dripping.

If it is slow to thicken but is approaching 210°F/100°C, remove the top portion of the double boiler and let it cool for a moment before returning to the heat for an additional minute or two of cooking. It typically takes 6 to 9 minutes for a curd to cook through.

When the curd has thickened to the consistency of sour cream, it is done. Remove the top half of the double boiler and stir off the heat. During this time, it will continue to thicken a bit.

Strain the curd through a fine-mesh sieve into a 4-cup/960 ml measure. The straining removes both the zest (which will have imparted a great deal of flavor to the curd during cooking time) and any bits of scrambled egg.

Pour the curd into the prepared jars, leaving a generous $\frac{1}{2}$ inch/12 mm of headspace. Wipe the rims, apply the lids and rings, and process in a boiling water bath for 25 minutes (see page 11).

When the time is up, remove the canning pot from the heat and remove the lid. Let the jars sit in the pot for an additional 5 minutes. This helps to prevent the curd from reacting to the rapid temperature change and bubbling out of the jars.

Meyer Lemon Curd

ZESTY LIME CURD

CONSIDER THIS LIME CURD THE CHEAPEST VACATION possible. For just a few dollars in ingredients and less than an hour of active work, I have a finished product that makes me feel transported to someplace tropical. Truly, after just a few tastes, the air seems to get warmer and I swear I can feel the grit of sand under my feet. Even if you don't need a beach escape, this curd is worth trying. I like to stir it into yogurt, but if you're searching for a more elegant application, try spreading it in a baked tart shell for a quick dessert. Top the tart with a ring of fresh raspberries if you really need to impress.

MAKES 2 (HALF-PINT/250 ML) JARS

$\frac{1}{4}$ cup/80 g finely grated lime zest (from about 4 limes)
1 $\frac{1}{4}$ cups/250 g granulated sugar
4 large egg yolks
2 large eggs
$\frac{1}{2}$ cup/120 ml freshly squeezed lime juice (from about 6 limes)
6 tablespoons/85 g cold unsalted butter, cut into cubes

Prepare a boiling water bath and 2 half-pint/250 ml jars according to the process on page 10. Place the lids in a small saucepan, cover them with water, and simmer over very low heat.

Combine the lime zest and sugar in a small bowl. Rub the zest into the sugar until it is fragrant and fully combined. Set aside.

Set up a double boiler, add 2 inches/5 cm of water to the bottom pan and bring to a simmer over medium heat. Alternatively, set a heatproof mixing bowl over a medium saucepan filled with 2 inches/5 cm of water, making sure the bottom of the bowl does not touch the surface of the water. Keeping the top half of the double boiler off the stove, add the egg yolks and whole eggs to it and whisk them together. Add the zest and sugar combination and whisk in. Finally, add the lime juice and stir until blended.

Put the double boiler back together and drop in the cubes of butter. Switch to a silicone spatula and stir continually as the lime curd cooks.

(continued)

Using a candy thermometer, monitor the temperature of the curd while you stir. As it approaches 190° to 200°F/90° to 95°C, it should start to thicken. One sign of doneness is that it will coat the back of your spatula without running or dripping.

If it is slow to thicken but is approaching 210°F/100°C, remove the top portion of the double boiler and let it cool for a moment before returning to the heat for an additional minute or two of cooking. It typically takes 6 to 9 minutes for a curd to cook through.

When the curd has thickened to the consistency of sour cream, it is done. Remove the top half of the double boiler and stir off the heat. During this time, it will continue to thicken a bit.

Strain the curd through a fine-mesh sieve into a 4-cup/960 ml measure. The straining removes both the zest (which will have imparted a great deal of flavor to the curd during cooking time) and any bits of scrambled egg.

Pour the curd into the prepared jars, leaving a generous ½ inch/12 mm of headspace. Wipe the rims, apply the lids and rings, and process in a boiling water bath canner for 25 minutes (see page 11).

When the time is up, remove the canning pot from the heat and remove the lid. Let the jars sit in the pot for an additional 5 minutes. This helps to prevent the curd from reacting to the rapid temperature change and bubbling out of the jars.

Note: If you prefer a curd shot through with flecks of zest, reserve half the zest at the beginning. After the curd is finished cooking and you've worked it through the sieve, add the reserved zest to the finished curd and stir to combine. This can be done with any of these curd recipes, but is particularly nice in the lime curd, as the green flecks gives a visual cue that you should expect the flavor of lime.

ORANGE VANILLA CURD

OKAY CREAMSICLE LOVERS, THIS ONE IS MOST DEC-cidedly for you. It recalls the frozen treats of our collective youth and transforms them into something best spread on homemade bis-cuits or a toasted English muffin. Because this recipe has a touch more liq-uid in it than the previous curd recipes, it will take just bit longer to thicken. Stick with it and keep stirring: You'll be well rewarded.

MAKES 2 (HALF-PINT/250 ML) JARS

1 $\frac{1}{4}$ cups/250 g sugar

$\frac{1}{4}$ cup/80 g orange zest (from about 3 oranges)

1 vanilla bean, split, scraped, and cut into $\frac{1}{2}$-inch/12 mm pieces

4 large egg yolks

2 large eggs

$\frac{1}{2}$ cup/120 ml freshly squeezed orange juice
   (from about 3 oranges)

2 tablespoons freshly squeezed lemon juice

6 tablespoons/85 g cold unsalted butter, cut into cubes

Prepare a boiling water bath and 2 half-pint/250 ml jars according to the process on page 10. Place the lids in a small saucepan, cover them with water, and simmer over very low heat.

In a small bowl, combine the sugar with the orange zest and vanilla bean and seeds. Rub the zest and vanilla into the sugar until it is fragrant and fully combined. Set aside.

Set up a double boiler, add 2 inches/5 cm of water to the bottom pan and bring to a simmer over medium heat. Alternatively, set a heatproof mixing bowl over a medium saucepan filled with 2 inches/5 cm of water, making sure the bottom of the bowl does not touch the surface of the water. Keeping the top half of the double boiler off the stove, add the egg yolks and whole eggs to it and whisk them together. Add the zest and sugar combination and whisk in. Finally, add the orange and lemon juices and stir until blended.

(continued)

Put the double boiler back together and drop in the cubes of butter. Switch to a silicone spatula and stir continually as the orange curd cooks.

Using a candy thermometer, monitor the temperature of the curd while you stir. As it approaches 190°F to 200°F/90°C to 95°C, it should start to thicken. One sign of doneness is that it will coat the back of the spatula without running or dripping.

If it is slow to thicken but is approaching 210°F/100°C, remove the top portion of the double boiler and let it cool for a moment before returning to the heat for an additional minute or two of cooking. It typically takes 10 to 12 minutes for this curd to cook through.

When the curd has thickened to the consistency of sour cream, it is done. Remove the top half of the double boiler and stir off the heat. During this time, it will continue to thicken a bit.

Strain the curd through a fine-mesh sieve into a 4-cup/960 ml measure. The straining removes both the zest (which will have imparted a great deal of flavor to the curd during cooking time) and any bits of scrambled egg. Pour the curd into the prepared jars. Wipe the rims and apply the lids and rings.

Because this curd is lower in acid than the others, you must keep this one stored in the refrigerator or freezer instead of putting it through a boiling water bath process. It will keep for up to a year in the freezer.

APPLE ALMOND
HONEY CONSERVE ᕦᕤ

THIS CONSERVE WAS ORIGINALLY INSPIRED BY charoses, a customary element of the Passover meal. No Passover Seder is complete without this salad of apples and walnuts, bound by honey and a splash of red wine. This version takes those traditional elements and translates them into a satisfying, not-too-sweet spread. What's more, you don't have to be Jewish to enjoy it. Try it with roasted meat or a side of runny cheese.

MAKES 5 (HALF-PINT/250 ML) JARS

8 cups peeled and chopped apples
   (about 4 pounds/1.8 kg apples; see note, page 47)
1 1/2 cups/360 ml 100-percent grape juice (no sugar added)
1 cup/240 ml honey
1 cup/200 g granulated sugar
2 1/2 teaspoons ground cinnamon
1/2 cup/70 g almonds, toasted and chopped

Prepare a boiling water bath and 5 half-pint/250 ml jars according to the process on page 10. Place the lids in a small saucepan, cover them with water, and simmer over very low heat.

Combine the apples and grape juice in a large, nonreactive pot. Cook over high heat for about 15 minutes, until the apples are tender and the liquid has reduced. Using an immersion blender or a potato masher, blend or mash about two-thirds of the apples. Leave the remaining third in chunks to give the finished conserve some texture.

Add the honey and sugar and continue to cook on high heat until it reaches 220°F/105°C, about 10 to15 minutes. This is a splattery recipe, so make sure to take care while cooking that you don't burn yourself. A mesh splatter screen is useful here.

When the conserve has reached 220°F/105°C, remove the pot from the heat and add the cinnamon and nuts. Stir to combine.

Ladle the conserve into the prepared jars, leaving a generous 1/2 inch/12 mm of headspace. Wipe the rims, apply the lids and rings, and process in a boiling water bath for 10 minutes (see page 11).

PEAR GINGER CONSERVE

THIS CONSERVE IS THE FIRST COUSIN OF THE PEAR Ginger Jam on page 46. The addition of chopped orange rind and walnut transforms it into a preserve that has a bit of kick and chew which complements a variety of cheeses. It also happens to be a divine spread on a slice of raisin-nut bread.

MAKES 2 (1-PINT/500 ML) JARS

6 cups cored and chopped Bartlett or Anjou pears (about 3 pounds/1.4 kg)

1 whole orange, seeded and finely chopped

3 cups/600 g granulated sugar

Zest and juice of 1 lemon

1 tablespoon grated peeled fresh ginger (from about one 2-inch/5 cm piece)

3/4 cup/85 g chopped walnuts

Prepare a boiling water bath and 2 regular-mouth 1-pint/500 ml jars according to the process on page 10. Place the lids in a small saucepan, cover them with water, and simmer over very low heat.

In a large nonreactive pot, combine the pears, chopped orange, and sugar. Bring to a simmer over medium-high heat. Add the lemon zest and juice and grated ginger and stir to combine.

Increase the heat and bring to a boil. Cook until the syrup turns translucent and the pears are soft enough that you can crush them with the back of your spoon, about 15-20 minutes.

Stir in the chopped walnuts and cook for an additional 5 minutes, stirring frequently.

Remove the pot from heat and ladle the conserve into the prepared jars, leaving ½ inch/12 mm headspace. Wipe the rims, apply the lids and rings, and process in a boiling water bath for 10 minutes (see page 11).

Pear-Ginger Conserve & Apple-Pear Chutney

CRANBERRY CONSERVE

WHEN I FIRST MADE THIS CONSERVE, I WASN'T sure what to do with it. It had the punchy bitterness of marmalade, but with the texture of a relish. However, soon enough, it had grown on me to the point where I couldn't imagine eating roast chicken without a dab. It's wonderful around the holidays, when most people have a surplus of baked ham and roast turkey.

MAKES 5 (HALF-PINT/250 ML) JARS

3 cups/300 g fresh cranberries
1 cup/240 ml orange juice
1 whole orange, seeded and finely chopped
1 tart apple (such as Granny Smith),
    peeled, cored, and minced
12 dried apricots, chopped
$\frac{1}{2}$ cup/120 ml honey
2 cups/400 g granulated sugar
$\frac{1}{2}$ cup/70 g slivered almonds
$\frac{1}{2}$ teaspoon ground ginger

Prepare a boiling water bath and 5 half-pint/250 ml jars according to the process on page 10. Place the lids in a small saucepan, cover them with water, and simmer over very low heat.

Combine the cranberries, orange juice, and chopped orange in a large, nonreactive pot. Bring to a simmer over medium-high heat and let cook until the cranberries begin to burst, about 10 minutes.

Add the chopped apple, apricots, honey, and sugar and increase the heat to high. Cook for about 20 minutes, until the orange rinds are tender and the mixture has thickened. When it reaches a thick, spreadable consistency, remove the pot from the heat and stir in the chopped almonds and ginger.

Ladle the conserve into the prepared jars, leaving $\frac{1}{2}$ inch/12 mm headspace. Wipe the rims, apply the lids and rings, and process in a boiling water bath for 10 minutes (see page 11).

CHUTNEYS & CONDIMENTS

DURING MY FIRST TEN YEARS OF LIFE, I HELD FAST to a strict condiment matrix. Mustard went on hot dogs. Ketchup belonged with hamburgers and French fries (meatloaf was also an acceptable vehicle). Mayonnaise was only good as a dipping sauce for steamed broccoli or asparagus. Salad dressing was Italian and made from a packet on which the words "Good Seasons" were emblazoned. Blueberry or plum jam went on buttered toast and honey went with peanut butter. Chutney, hot sauce, and relish didn't exist for me.

As I got older, I became aware of the wider world of condiments and my matrix started to crumble. The introduction of soy and teriyaki sauces caused the initial cracks and sweet red chili sauce dealt the final blow.

Now I'm an equal opportunity condiment user and the bulk of the precious real estate on our refrigerator door is devoted to housing the assorted bottles and jars (sadly, my husband is still strictly a ketchup and Thousand Island dressing guy).

Here are just a couple of tips as you tackle these condiment recipes. Chutneys and ketchups will always take longer to cook down than you might think possible. They also need more stirring than you might think reasonable, so stay close and plan for other kitchen projects to keep you occupied as you wait for them to thicken.

Mustards are incredibly easy to make, but just like pickles, they need a chunk of time to cure before they'll be ready to eat. Don't be discouraged if your mustard is both bitter and bland at first. I promise it will age into something worthy of that artisanal sausage.

Finally, if you plan on taking a chutney to a potluck or party, I recommend opening it at least an hour prior to serving. Just like wine, chutney needs a bit of time to breathe. Otherwise, all you'll taste is the vinegar.

RHUBARB CHUTNEY

THIS CHUTNEY MAKES AN EXCELLENT POTLUCK CONtribution when paired with a log of goat cheese and a tender baguette. It's adapted from the rhubarb chutney recipe in *The New York Times Heritage Cookbook* that was printed in 1971 and edited by Jean Hewitt.

MAKES 3 (1-PINT/500 ML) JARS

6 cups sliced rhubarb (about 2 pounds/910 kg rhubarb stalks)

3 cups/345 g sliced onion (2 medium onions)

1 cup/170 g raisins

3 cups/600 g (packed) light brown sugar

2 cups/480 ml apple cider vinegar

1 tablespoon salt

1 teaspoon ground cinnamon

1 teaspoon ground ginger

$\frac{1}{2}$ teaspoon mustard seed

$\frac{1}{2}$ teaspoon ground cloves

$\frac{1}{2}$ teaspoon red pepper flakes

$\frac{1}{8}$ teaspoon cayenne pepper

Prepare a boiling water bath and 3 regular-mouth 1-pint/500 ml jars according to the process on page 10. Place the lids in a small saucepan, cover them with water, and simmer over very low heat.

Combine all ingredients in a large pot and bring to a boil. Reduce the heat and simmer gently until the mixture is thick and sticky, stirring regularly for 45 to 75 minutes. You'll know it's done when all the ingredients have come together in a uniformly brown mash (chutney always tastes better than it looks).

When the chutney is finished cooking, ladle it into the prepared jars, leaving $\frac{1}{2}$ inch/12 mm of headspace. Wipe the rims, apply the lids and rings, and process in a boiling water bath for 15 minutes (see page 11).

Note: The cooking times for chutneys can vary drastically depending on the width of your pot, the amount of humidity in the air, and the water content of the ingredients. The goal is to cook it down until it is thick and any remaining liquid is syrupy. Give it plenty of time and stir it regularly to ensure that it does not burn.

SPICY TOMATO CHUTNEY

A COUPLE SUMMERS AGO, I PROMISED TO TEACH A canning class in which we'd make a spicy tomato chutney. At the time, of course, I had no such recipe and so spent the weeks before the class making a progression of batches before hitting upon a winner. This one, with its Indian-inspired palette of flavors was far and away the most delicious and interesting. Now, I make it each year for nibbling and gift giving.

MAKES 3 (1-PINT/500 ML) JARS

2 teaspoons mustard seed (brown or black)

2 teaspoons fennel seed

2 teaspoons celery seed

1 teaspoon coriander seed

$\frac{1}{8}$ teaspoon cayenne pepper

$2\frac{1}{2}$ cups/600 ml distilled white vinegar

2 cups/400 g granulated sugar

5 pounds/2.3 kg plum or Roma tomatoes, peeled, cored, and chopped (see page 164 for peeling instructions)

1 teaspoon salt

In a dry skillet, toast together the mustard, fennel, celery, and coriander seeds over medium heat until they begin to pop and smell fragrant, about 3 minute. Pour the seeds into a small bowl and combine with the cayenne. Set aside.

In a large pot, combine the vinegar and sugar and simmer over high heat until the sugar dissolves. Add the tomatoes and the seeds. Stir to combine and bring to a boil. Reduce heat to medium and cook, stirring often, until the tomatoes have reduced and developed a thick, spreadable consistency, about 1 to $1\frac{1}{2}$ hours.

After the chutney has cooked for approximately 45 minutes to 1 hour, prepare a boiling water bath and 3 regular-mouth 1-pint/500 ml jars according to the process on page 10. Place the lids in a small saucepan, cover with water, and bring to a simmer over very low heat.

When the chutney is finished cooking, ladle it into the prepared jars, leaving $\frac{1}{2}$ inch/12 mm of headspace. Wipe the rims, apply the lids and rings, and process in a boiling water bath for 15 minutes (see page 11).

GREEN TOMATO CHUTNEY

I DREAMED UP THIS CHUTNEY ONE FALL WHEN MY community garden tomato plants were heavy with green fruit and the days were rapidly getting shorter. My parents tend to harvest their green tomatoes and slowly let them ripen in cardboard boxes in their garage. However, living in a 1,100 square foot apartment means I don't have the same luxury of space. So, after reading every chutney recipe I had, I cobbled this one together. It's good with cheddar cheese and great alongside scrambled eggs.

MAKES 2 (1-PINT/500 ML) JARS

6 cups chopped green tomato (about 3 pounds/1.4 kg)

1¼ cups/200 g chopped yellow onion

1 cup/240 ml apple cider vinegar

1½ cups/300 g (packed) brown sugar

2 teaspoons ground ginger

1 teaspoon sea salt

½ teaspoon ground cloves

¼ teaspoon red pepper flakes

2 cinnamon sticks

3 whole star anise

2 tablespoons finely chopped crystallized ginger

Prepare a boiling water bath and 2 regular-mouth 1-pint/500 ml jars according to the process on page 10. Place the lids in a small saucepan, cover them with water, and simmer over very low heat.

Combine all ingredients except the crystallized ginger in a large pot and bring to a boil. Reduce the heat and simmer, stirring regularly, until the chutney is thick and any remaining liquid looks syrupy, not watery, about 1 to 1½ hours.

When the chutney is finished cooking, stir in the chopped crystallized ginger. Ladle the chutney into the prepared jars, leaving ½ inch/12 mm of headspace. Wipe the rims, apply the lids and rings, and process in a boiling water bath for 15 minutes (see page 11).

APPLE-PEAR CHUTNEY

THIS CHUTNEY IS LOOSELY BASED ON THE PEACH chutney that my friend Audra has been making for years. In the summer of 2009, she posted it on her wonderful blog, Doris and Jilly Cook. Her original peach version is so spectacular that I made this version featuring fall fruit. I think it's the whole chopped lemon that makes it so special.

MAKES 4 (1-PINT/500 ML) JARS

3 pounds/1.4 kg apples (about 8 to 10 apples)

2 pounds/910 g thin-skinned pears, such as Bartlett or Anjou (about 5 to 6 pears)

3 cups/510 g dark raisins

2 cups/320 g chopped yellow onion (about 2 medium onions)

1 lemon, seeded and finely minced with peel

$2\frac{1}{2}$ cups/600 ml apple cider vinegar

4 cups/800 g (packed) light brown sugar

2 tablespoons mustard seed

3 whole cloves

2 cinnamon sticks

2 teaspoons red pepper flakes

5 garlic cloves, chopped

1 (3-inch/7.5 cm) piece fresh ginger, peeled and grated

Combine all ingredients in a large pot, stir to combine, and bring to a vigorous boil. Reduce the heat to medium and cook, stirring often, until the mixture has reduced and developed a thick, spreadable consistency, about 2 hours.

After the chutney has cooked for approximately $1\frac{1}{2}$ hours, prepare a boiling water bath and 4 regular-mouth 1-pint/500 ml jars. Place the lids in a small saucepan, cover them with water, and bring to a simmer over very low heat.

When the chutney is finished cooking, remove the cinnamon sticks and discard. Ladle the chutney into the prepared jars, leaving $\frac{1}{2}$ inch/12 mm of headspace. Wipe the rims, apply the lids and rings, and process in a boiling water bath for 15 minutes (see page 11).

TOMATO KETCHUP

IF YOU ARE A KETCHUP LOVER, I HIGHLY RECOMMEND taking a stab at making your own. If nothing else, it will give you an appreciation for just how many tomatoes go into every puddle of ketchup you squirt on a burger or plate of french fries. It will also give you a chance to customize it to your liking so that whether you're looking to increase the heat or decrease the sweetness, you can do it with ease.

MAKES 6 (HALF-PINT/250 ML) JARS

8 pounds/3.6 kg chopped Roma or paste tomatoes
1 cup/160 g chopped yellow onion (about 1 medium onion)
$\frac{1}{2}$ cup/75 g chopped red bell pepper (about $\frac{1}{2}$ pepper)
2 cups/480 ml cider vinegar
$\frac{3}{4}$ cup/150 g (packed) light brown sugar
1 teaspoon celery seed
$\frac{1}{4}$ teaspoon cayenne pepper
1 teaspoon whole cloves
1 teaspoon mustard seed
1 teaspoon whole allspice
1 cinnamon stick, crushed

Prepare a boiling water bath and 6 half-pint/250 ml jars according to the process on page 10. Place the lids in a small saucepan, cover them with water, and simmer over very low heat.

Combine the tomatoes, onion, and red bell peppers in a large pot. Bring to a boil and then reduce temperature to medium. Cook until the vegetables are completely soft, about 30 minutes.

Position a sieve or food mill over a large bowl and press the tomato mixture through it. Discard the seeds and skins in the sieve and return the pulp to the pot.

Add the cider vinegar, brown sugar, celery seed, and cayenne pepper to the pot. Combine the cloves, mustard seed, allspice, and crushed cinnamon stick in a spice bag or tea ball, or bundle them in a piece of cheesecloth and secure tightly with kitchen twine and add to the pot.

Simmer over medium-low heat, stirring regularly, until the mixture has reduced by half and is quite thick, about 60 to 90 minutes.

When the ketchup is finished cooking, remove the spice bundle and discard. Ladle the ketchup into the prepared jars, leaving ½ inch/12 mm of headspace. Wipe the rims, apply the lids and rings, and process in a boiling water bath for 10 minutes (see page 11).

Note: If you're stumped about how to best crush a cinnamon stick, simply place it in a brown paper bag and fold the top of the bag several times so that it doesn't burst open. Give it several good whacks with a meat tenderizing mallet or rolling pin. It should break the cinnamon up into bits and pieces.

GRAPE KETCHUP

BACK IN THE DAYS BEFORE BIG COMPANIES RAN our food system, ketchup was made from of all manner of fruit. It's only in the last few generations that tomatoes won out as the primary ingredient. However, I've found that it's valuable to explore some of the older variations, even if just to appreciate the creativity of days gone past. If you tackle this recipe be warned that it won't taste exactly like your beloved Heinz. It's closer to barbecue sauce and I've often used it on pulled pork or brushed on grilled chicken legs.

MAKES 3 (1-PINT/500 ML) JARS

3 pounds/1.4 kg seedless red grapes (see note)
3 cups/720 ml apple cider vinegar
6 cups/1.2 kg granulated sugar
2 tablespoons ground cinnamon
2 teaspoons ground cloves
1 teaspoon dry mustard
¼ teaspoon cayenne pepper

Prepare a boiling water bath and 3 regular-mouth (1-pint/500 ml) jars according to the process on page 10. Place the lids in a small saucepan, cover them with water, and
(continued)

simmer over very low heat.

In a large pot, combine the grapes, cider vinegar, and sugar and bring to a boil. Reduce the heat to a bare simmer and cook for 30 minutes. After 30 minutes, check on the grapes and if there are some that have not broken down, mash them against the side of pot with a wooden spoon.

Add the cinnamon, cloves, dry mustard, and cayenne pepper and continue to cook for another 30 to 45 minutes, until the ketchup is thick and spreadable.

When the ketchup is finished cooking, ladle it into the prepared jars, leaving $\frac{1}{2}$ inch/12 mm of headspace. Wipe the rims, apply the lids and rings, and process in a boiling water bath for 10 minutes (see page 11).

Note: Because of availability, I use conventional, seedless grapes to make this recipe. However, it can be made with seedy backyard grapes. If you choose to use them, simmer the grapes with the vinegar and sugar as instructed. Once they've softened, position a food mill over a large bowl and press the grapes through, so that you separate the flesh of the grapes from the skins and seeds. Return the grape pulp to the pot, add the spices and proceed with the rest of the recipe.

CRANBERRY KETCHUP

I THINK IT'S HIGH TIME TO LIBERATE THE CRANBERRY from holiday sauces and juice drinks. This ketchup shows off the cranberry's sassy, savory side. Cranberries have a good deal of pectin, so be prepared for this ketchup to develop a firmer texture more quickly than the other ketchup recipes here. I often spread this condiment on sandwiches in place of mustard and it can be used as an easy, fruity marinade when thinned with some vinegar.

MAKES 6 (HALF-PINT/250 ML) JARS

4 pounds/1.8 kg fresh cranberries

2½ cups/400 g chopped yellow onion
  (about 2 medium onions)

2 cups/480 apple cider vinegar

4 cups/800 g (packed) light brown sugar

1 tablespoon salt

1 teaspoon freshly ground black pepper

1 tablespoon whole cloves

2 cinnamon sticks, crushed

1 tablespoon allspice berries

1 tablespoon celery seed

Prepare a boiling water bath and 6 half-pint/250 ml jars according to the process on page 10. Place the lids in a small saucepan, cover them with water, and simmer over very low heat.

Combine the cranberries, onions, and 4 cups/960 ml water in a large pot. Bring to a boil, reduce the temperature to medium and cook until the cranberries pop and the onions are soft, about 25 minutes.

Position a food mill or sieve over a large pot or bowl and press the cranberries and onions through. Discard the seeds and the skins in the food mill and return the pulp to the pot.

Add the cider vinegar, brown sugar, salt, and pepper to the pot. Combine the cloves, crushed cinnamon sticks, allspice berries, and celery seed in a spice bag or tea ball, or bundle them in a piece of cheesecloth and secure tightly with kitchen twine and add to the pot. Simmer over medium-low heat, stirring regularly, until the mixture is quite thick, about 30 minutes.

When the ketchup is finished cooking, remove the spice bundle and discard. Ladle the ketchup into the prepared jars, leaving ½ inch/12 mm of headspace. Wipe the rims, apply the lids and rings, and process in a boiling water bath for 10 minutes (see page 11).

GRAINY WHITE
WINE MUSTARD

I USED TO BE A HOPELESS CHUMP IN THE CONDIMENT
section of gourmet markets. I could not resist the squat jars of fancy
mustards, happily handing over $7 and $8 for the privilege of taking
them home. That all ended when I encountered Kaela Porter, who writes
the blog Local Kitchen. She has an innate gift for mustards and taught me
just how easy it could be to make those fancy spreads at home. Here's hop-
ing this recipe will be as liberating for you as Kaela's many mustards were
for me!

MAKES 3 (HALF-PINT/250 ML) JARS

$\frac{1}{2}$ cup/90 g yellow mustard seeds

$\frac{1}{4}$ cup/45 g brown mustard seeds

1 cup/240 ml dry white wine

1 cup/240 ml apple cider vinegar

$\frac{1}{3}$ cup/65 g (packed) light brown sugar

1 tablespoon garlic powder

1 teaspoon onion powder

$\frac{1}{2}$ teaspoon freshly ground black pepper

$\frac{1}{2}$ teaspoon sea salt

1 teaspoon grated lemon zest

Combine both mustard seeds and the wine in a medium pot and bring to a boil.
Remove from the heat. Cover the pot and allow the seeds to sit 2 to 12 hours, until all
the liquid has been absorbed.

Prepare a boiling water bath and 3 half-pint/250 ml jars according to the process
on page 10. Place the lids in a small saucepan, cover them with water, and simmer
over very low heat.

Transfer the seeds and any remaining liquid to a blender or food processor. Add 1
cup/240 ml water and blend or process until the seeds are fairly well broken down,
though the amount of blending you do is entirely up to the texture you prefer.

Transfer processed seeds back to the pot in which they were soaked. Add the cider vinegar, brown sugar, garlic powder, onion powder, black pepper, sea salt, and lemon zest and whisk to combine.

Bring the mustard to a boil, then reduce the heat and simmer until it reduces and thickens a bit, about 10 minutes.

Ladle the mustard into the prepared jars, leaving ½ inch/12 mm of headspace. Wipe the rims, apply the lids and rings, and process in a boiling water bath for 15 minutes (see page 11).

SPICY HONEY MUSTARD

THE FIRST TIME YOU MAKE MUSTARD AT HOME, you'll look at it when it's all done and think, "That's it?" Yep, that's really it. It's one of the easiest things to do in your kitchen; once you get started, you won't be able to stop. This particular mustard is smooth and spicy and will remind you of the hot mustard served at Chinese restaurants. The heat will mellow with time, so if you prefer a highly spiced mustard, eat it sooner. I like this one with sausages that have a higher fat content, as all that good grease plays nicely with heat.

MAKES 4 (QUARTER-PINT/125 ML) JARS

1 cup/90 g dry mustard
1 cup/240 ml cider vinegar
⅓ cup/75 ml honey
½ teaspoon salt
¼ teaspoon freshly ground black pepper

Prepare a boiling water bath and 4 quarter-pint/125 ml jars according to the process on page 10. Place the lids in a small saucepan, cover them with water, and simmer over very low heat.

Combine all ingredients in a small pot. Whisk to blend and bring to a simmer over medium heat for 5-6 minutes. When the mustard is thoroughly heated through, ladle it into the prepared jars, leaving ½ inch/12 mm of headspace. Wipe the rims, apply the lids and rings, and process in a boiling water bath for 10 minutes (see page 11).

PICKLES

I GREW UP IN A HOUSEHOLD THAT APPRECIATED ITS pickles. As a kid, one of my favorite after-school snacks was a garlicky cucumber dill, fished from the jar using a fork and two fingers. I'd slowly nibble away at the pickle over my book of the moment, until all I had left was the stem end of the cucumber and wrinkly, vinegar-scented fingers.

As a child, I was taught by my parents that there are hard-and-fast rules regarding the construction of a quality sandwich. An essential tenet of this philosophy is that no good sandwich is complete without an interior layer of thinly sliced sour pickles, blotted almost dry. Thanks to this early conditioning, I cannot be satisfied by a sandwich that does not include a tart, crunchy component.

In recent years, I've spent time exploring the world beyond the cucumber pickle and have discovered that there are few vegetables that don't appreciate liberal applications of vinegar, salt, and spices. Of all the pickles I make, I think my very favorite is the rarely-found-in-grocery-stores dilly bean. Green beans have the internal fortitude to stand up to the heat of a boiling water bath and retain an amazing crispness even many months after they are made. I particularly like placing a few alongside a hot dog at summer cookouts.

Before you dig into the recipes in this section, there are a few things you should know. One is that the salt is included in these recipes because it helps with the preservation of the vegetable. I know it may seem like a lot, but it's vital to the integrity of the recipe. Please don't reduce it.

You'll notice that some of these recipes call for just five minutes of time in the boiling water bath. This shorter processing time helps maintain the crisp texture of the finished pickle. However, when you process for less than ten minutes, you have to make sure you're working with sterilized jars. To do this, boil the jars in your canner for at least ten minutes prior to packing and filling.

Remove the jars from the canner just before you're ready to fill them to help preserve their state of hyper cleanliness.

You'll find that a large part of your pickle success will depend on the jars you choose. I've found that regular-mouth jars work better for pickles than wide-mouth jars. This is because the shoulders of regular-mouth jars help keep the pickles submerged in the brine. A wide-mouth jar has no narrowing sides that prevent your vegetables from floating. While there isn't anything essentially wrong with a floating pickle (it happens to the best of us), fully submerged pickles are more immune to discoloration and reduction in quality. Plus, they just look better.

To make the brine, all of these recipes work with a ratio of one part vinegar to one part water. To ensure a safe product, you must start with vinegar that has been diluted so that its acidity is 5 percent. Most commercial vinegars will say this on the package, but it's important to check to be safe. This does mean that using homemade or artisanal vinegars is not recommended for pickles that you plan on canning for shelf stability.

Many of these recipes will direct you to "bubble" your jars after filling them but before sealing them. This is a process in which you either tap the jar gently on a towel-lined countertop or use a wooden chopstick to help dislodge any trapped pockets of air. You want to remove these bubbles before putting the lids on the jars, as they'll then try to escape during the boiling water bath process and will take some of your brine with them. The reason to use a wooden implement is that it greatly reduces the risk that you'll scratch the interior of your jar. Over time, scratches made by metal utensils can wear down the jars and lead to breakage.

MIXED PICKLING SPICE

YOU CAN BUY READY-MADE PICKLING SPICE FROM a variety of outlets and manufacturers and many of them are excellent. I like to mix my own so that I can customize the blend of flavors. As you spend some time making and eating your pickles, you can adjust the amounts to please your palate. The proportions I particularly like are listed below. However, if making your own pickling spice feels like a daunting task, feel free to use a pre-blended mix. I like the one that Penzeys Spices (penzeys.com) makes.

**MAKES ENOUGH FOR ABOUT 20
(1-PINT/500 ML) JARS OF PICKLES**

3 tablespoons crushed bay leaves
3 tablespoons black peppercorns
3 tablespoons whole allspice
3 tablespoons coriander seeds
3 tablespoons mustard seeds
3 tablespoons juniper berries
1 tablespoon whole cloves
1 tablespoon dill seed
1 cinnamon stick, broken into pieces

Pour all the spices into a jar, seal, and shake to combine. Use any time a mixed pickling spice is called for.

PICKLED GARLIC SCAPES

GARLIC SCAPES ARE THE CURLY GREEN SHOOT THAT all garlic plants send out come springtime. They get chopped off so that the plants can focus all their energy into the development of bulbs. Scapes used to be something that farmers discarded or kept for their own use, but they started appearng at farmers' markets a few years ago. They have the crunch of a string bean, but with a light garlic flavor.

MAKES 2 (1-PINT/500 ML) JARS

1 $^1/_2$ cups/360 ml apple cider vinegar
2 tablespoons pickling salt
1 $^1/_2$ pounds/680 g garlic scapes
2 tablespoons Mixed Pickling Spice (page 118), divided
$^1/_2$ teaspoon red pepper flakes, divided

Prepare a boiling water bath and 2 wide mouth 1-pint/500 ml jars according to the process on page 10. Place the lids in a small saucepan, cover them with water, and simmer over very low heat.

Combine the vinegar, 1 $^1/_2$ cups/360 ml water, and pickling salt in a pot and bring the brine to a boil.

Meanwhile, trim the ends of the scapes, both the blossom end and the hard bit that formed at the original cut, and cut them into lengths that will fit in your jars.

Add 1 tablespoon pickling spice and $^1/_4$ teaspoon red pepper flakes to each sterilized jar. Pack the trimmed scapes into the jars.

Slowly pour the hot brine over the garlic scapes in each jar, leaving $^1/_2$ inch/12 mm headspace. Gently tap the jars on a towel-lined countertop to help loosen any bubbles before using a wooden chopstick to dislodge any remaining bubbles. Check the headspace again and add more brine if necessary.

Wipe the rims, apply the lids and rings, and process in a hot water bath for 10 minutes (see page 11).

Let these pickles cure for at least 1 week before eating.

Note: I like to stack the curly parts of the garlic scapes along the jar walls and then pack the straighter ends upright inside. It ends up looking like a curly log cabin, which always appeals to me.

PICKLED ASPARAGUS SPEARS ∼2

I N THE YEARS BEFORE I DISCOVERED THE FLAVOR
miracle that is pickled asparagus, I would spend each asparagus season in an eating frenzy, motivated by the hope that I'd be able to satisfy
a year's worth of vegetal desire in just three weeks. While I still eat more
than my share while it's in the farmers' markets, I've channeled some of my
maniacal asparagus energy into putting some up for the rest of the year.
They make particularly good stirrers for a homemade Bloody Mary.

MAKES 3 (1-PINT/500 ML) JARS

4 pounds/1.8 kg asparagus
3 cups/720 ml cider vinegar
3 tablespoons pickling salt
3 lemon slices
3 tablespoons Mixed Pickling Spice (page 118), divided
1 ½ teaspoons red pepper flakes, divided
3 garlic cloves, peeled

Prepare a boiling water bath and 4 regular-mouth 1-pint/500 ml jars according to the
process on page 10. Place the lids in a small saucepan, cover them with water, and
simmer over very low heat.

Wash the asparagus and trim the ends so that the spears will fit in your jars with ½
inch/12 mm of headspace. Bring a large pot of water to a boil and, working in
batches, blanch the trimmed asparagus for 10 seconds. As it comes out of the boiling water, put the asparagus into a large bowl of ice water to stop the cooking. The
asparagus should be a bright, verdant green at this point.

Combine the vinegar, pickling salt, and 3 cups/720 ml water in a pot and bring the
brine to a boil.

Meanwhile, remove the jars from the hot water. Put a lemon slice in the bottom of
each jar. Add 1 tablespoon pickling spice and ½ teaspoon red pepper flakes to each
jar. Pack in the trimmed and blanched asparagus (it's up to you to determine whether
you want to go tips up or down). Tuck 1 garlic clove down into each jar.

Slowly pour the hot brine over the asparagus spears in each jar, leaving ½ inch/12 mm headspace. Gently tap the jars on a towel-lined countertop to help loosen any bubbles before using a wooden chopstick to dislodge any remaining bubbles. Check the headspace again and add more brine if necessary.

Wipe the rims, apply the lids and rings, and process in a boiling water bath for 10 minutes (see page 11).

Wait at least 24 hours before eating, to give the asparagus spears a chance to get absorb the brine. They will continue to get increasingly delicious over time.

Note: The only tricky thing about pickling asparagus is finding the best jars for the job. I like the taller, 12-ounce/360 ml jelly jars that Ball makes, as they allow you to include a bit more stalk length. Last year, I also invested in a six-pack of the tall cylindrical jars that Weck designed particularly for this task. They are fabulous and I highly recommend them.

DILLY BEANS

THIS IS ONE OF MY FAVORITE PICKLES. I'VE ALWAYS been a string bean lover, so I may have an innate bias. I can easily decimate an entire pint in an afternoon, eating them out of the jar until all that's left is a bobbing garlic clove. They stay incredibly crisp after many months on the shelf. When I'm not eating them straight from the fridge, I like them chopped up in tuna salad or on a cheese plate.

MAKES 4 (1-PINT/500 ML) JARS

2 pounds/910 g green beans
$2\frac{1}{2}$ cups/600 ml distilled white vinegar
$\frac{1}{4}$ cup/50 g pickling salt
1 teaspoon cayenne pepper
4 teaspoons dill seed (not dill weed)
4 garlic cloves, peeled

Prepare a boiling water bath and 4 regular-mouth 1-pint/500 ml jars according to the process on page 10. Place the lids in a small saucepan, cover them with water, and simmer over very low heat.

Wash and trim the beans so that they fit in your jars. Combine the vinegar, $2\frac{1}{2}$ cups/600 ml water, and pickling salt in a pot and bring the brine to a boil.

Meanwhile, pack the beans into the sterilized jars, leaving $\frac{1}{2}$ inch/12 mm headspace. Add $\frac{1}{4}$ teaspoon cayenne pepper (more if you're a lover of heat), 1 garlic clove, and 1 teaspoon dill seeds to each jar.

Slowly pour the hot brine over the beans in each jar, leaving $\frac{1}{2}$ inch/12 mm headspace. Gently tap the jars on a towel-lined countertop to help loosen any bubbles before using a wooden chopstick to dislodge any remaining bubbles. Check the headspace again and add more brine if necessary.

Wipe the rims, apply the lids and rings, and process in a boiling water bath for 5 minutes (see page 11).

Let these pickles cure for at least 2 weeks before eating.

Note: If you have easy access to dill heads, feel free to substitute them for the dill seed called for in this recipe. I wouldn't, however, recommend using fronds of dill weed, as they can break down during storage and turn the brine murky.

PICKLED OKRA

DURING MY EARLY CANNING DAYS, I SPENT A WEEK in Austin, Texas. It was there that I had the chance to try the most delectable fried okra I'd ever encountered. It transformed my opinion of this sometimes texturally challenging vegetable and sent me running to the kitchen to try it as a pickle. It was transcendently good. Pickling manages to eradicate the interior slime and just leaves you with a crunchy, brine-filled pickle. It's a dream eaten alongside a plate of spicy food.

MAKES 4 (1-PINT/500 ML) JARS

3 cups/720 ml apple cider vinegar
3 tablespoons pickling salt
4 lemon slices
4 tablespoons Mixed Pickling Spice (page 118), divided
2 pounds/910 g okra, washed and trimmed
4 garlic cloves, peeled

Prepare a boiling water bath and 4 regular-mouth 1-pint/500 ml jars according to the process on page 10. Place the lids in a small saucepan, cover them with water, and simmer over very low heat.

Combine the vinegar, 3 cups/720 ml water, and pickling salt in a pot and bring the brine to a boil.

Meanwhile, put a lemon slice and 1 tablespoon pickling spice in the bottom of each sterilized jar. Then pack the okra in, first laying them in so that the points are up. Then insert another layer with the points down, so that they interlock. Nestle 1 garlic clove among the okra in each jar.

Slowly pour the hot brine over the okra in each jar, leaving ½ inch/12 mm headspace. Gently tap the jars on a towel-lined countertop to help loosen any bubbles before using a wooden chopstick to dislodge any remaining bubbles. Check the headspace again and add more brine if necessary.

Wipe the rims, apply the lids and rings, and process in a boiling water bath for 10 minutes (see page 11).

Let these pickles cure for at least 1 week before eating.

Note: You'll find that this recipe calls for you to make more brine than many of the other similarly scaled recipes. Because okra pods are hollow, they will absorb a great deal of the brine. When you've finished filling and bubbling all the jars, they will invariably require topping off. What's more, the brine level will drop radically after you remove the jars from the canner: Do not be alarmed. The brine has simply migrated inside the okra pods. There is no need to remove the lids to top off the liquid; as long as the seal is good, they are safe to store and eat.

CLASSIC DILL PICKLES

THESE PICKLES ARE AS CLOSE AS I'VE BEEN ABLE to get to the chunky dills of my childhood. They are tangy, garlicky, and a little bit spicy. If I'm able to find smaller pickling cucumbers, I will pack them into the jars whole, as they stay crisper that way. But often, the only pickle-appropriate cukes I can find are quite large, making it necessary to cut them down to get them into the jars. If you're using sliced cucumbers, do your best to stick to the 5-minute processing time, to minimize the softening effects that the boiling water can have.

MAKES 4 (1-PINT/500 ML) JARS

2 cups/480 ml apple cider vinegar

3 teaspoons pickling salt

8 garlic cloves, peeled

1 teaspoon red pepper flakes, divided

4 teaspoons dill seed, divided

2 teaspoons black peppercorns, divided

1 (overflowing) pint/600 g pickling cucumbers,
　left whole or sliced into spears

Prepare a boiling water bath and 4 regular-mouth 1-pint/500 ml jars according to the process on page 10. Place the lids in a small saucepan, cover them with water, and simmer over very low heat.

Combine the vinegar, 2 cups/480 ml water, and pickling salt in a pot and bring the brine to a boil.

Add 2 garlic cloves, $\frac{1}{4}$ teaspoon red pepper flakes, 1 teaspoon dill seed, and $\frac{1}{2}$ teaspoon black peppercorns to each sterilized jar. Trim off the blossom end of the cucumbers and pack them firmly into the jars. You don't want to damage the cukes, but you do want them packed tightly.

Slowly pour the hot brine over the cucumbers in each jar, leaving $\frac{1}{2}$ inch/12 mm headspace. Gently tap the jars on a towel-lined countertop to help loosen any bubbles before using a wooden chopstick to dislodge any remaining bubbles. Check the headspace again and add more brine if necessary.

Wipe the rims, apply the lids and rings, and process in a boiling water bath for 5 minutes (see page 11).

Let these pickles cure for at least 1 week before eating.

Note: Make sure to stick with pickling cucumbers (also called Kirby cucumbers) for this recipe. Using other cucumbers will often result in a disappointing pickle, as they don't hold their structure as well. Also, don't skip trimming off the blossom end. It contains an enzyme that can lead to limp pickles.

PICKLED ZUCCHINI

I HAVE A GO-TO SLAW RECIPE THAT CONSISTS OF SHR-
edded cabbage tossed in a vinaigrette of lime juice, olive oil, and a generous heap of cumin. One summer, awash in squash, I was determined to
translate that dressing into brine. This tasty pickle was the happy result.

MAKES 4 (1-PINT/500 ML) JARS

3 pounds/1.4 kg young zucchini,
   sliced into rounds $\frac{1}{2}$ inch/12 mm thick
2 cups/480 ml apple cider vinegar
3 teaspoons ground cumin
3 tablespoons pickling salt
1 lime, sliced
2 teaspoons black peppercorns, divided
1 teaspoon cumin seed, divided
1 teaspoon mustard seed, divided
1 teaspoon red pepper flakes, divided

Prepare a boiling water bath and 4 regular-mouth 1-pint/500 ml jars according to the
process on page 10. Place the lids in a small saucepan, cover them with water, and
simmer over very low heat.

Combine the vinegar, 2 cups/480 ml water, ground cumin, and pickling salt in a pot
and bring the brine to a boil.

Meanwhile, place a lime slice in the bottom of each sterilized jar. Add $\frac{1}{2}$ teaspoon
peppercorns, $\frac{1}{4}$ teaspoon cumin seed, $\frac{1}{4}$ teaspoon mustard seed, and $\frac{1}{4}$ teaspoon
red pepper flakes to each jar.

Pack the sliced zucchini into each jar. Slowly pour the hot brine over the zucchini in
each jar, leaving $\frac{1}{2}$ inch/12 mm headspace. Gently tap the jars on a towel-lined
countertop to help loosen any bubbles before using a wooden chopstick to dislodge
any remaining bubbles. Use a wooden chopstick to work the air bubbles out of the
jars. Check the headspace again and add more brine if necessary.

Wipe the rims, apply the lids and rings, and process in a hot water bath for 10 minutes (see page 11).

Note: It is particularly vital here that your cumin is potent. As it ages, cumin can turn
muddy; making for decidedly lackluster pickles.

BREAD-AND-BUTTER PICKLES

READ SOMEWHERE THAT THE NAME "BREAD-AND-butter pickle" is a remnant of leaner days. When a family lacked the means to purchase more exalted sandwich fillings, they'd turn to jars of homemade sweet pickles to round out a meal of bread and butter. Whether or not the story is true, I do find that these pickles are excellent both as sandwich topper and as a straight-from-the-jar snack. For unabashed dedication to authenticity, search out a knife or mandoline designed to make crinkle cuts.

MAKES 5 (1-PINT/500 ML) JARS

6 cups thickly sliced pickling cucumbers
 (about 1 quart/1 kg whole cucumbers)
2 cups sliced red bell peppers (about 2 peppers)
2 cups sliced onion (about 1 large onion)
1/4 cup/50 g pickling salt
2 cups/480 ml apple cider vinegar
1 1/2 cups/300 g granulated sugar
2 tablespoons mustard seed
2 teaspoons celery seed
1 teaspoon red pepper flakes
1/2 teaspoon ground cloves

Combine the sliced cucumbers, bell peppers, onion, and pickling salt in a large bowl. Place them in the refrigerator and let them sit for between 4 and 12 hours. The goal is to draw as much liquid out of the cucumbers as possible (so it can later be replaced with the brine). Rinse and drain the vegetables.

Prepare a boiling water bath and 5 regular-mouth 1-pint/500 ml jars according to the process on page 10. Place the lids in a small saucepan, cover them with water, and simmer over very low heat.

Combine the vinegar and sugar in a large pot. Heat over medium heat until the sugar is dissolved. Add the mustard seed, celery seed, red pepper flakes and cloves. Increase the heat to high and bring the brine to a boil. Add the drained vegetables

(continued)

and stir to combine. Cook for 5 minutes, until all the vegetables in the brine are fully heated through.

Using tongs, fill the sterilized jars with the vegetables. Slowly pour the hot brine over the vegetables in each jar, leaving ½ inch/12 mm headspace. Gently tap the jars on a towel-lined countertop to help loosen any bubbles before using a wooden chopstick to dislodge any remaining bubbles. Check the headspace again and add more brine if necessary.

Wipe the rims, apply the lids and rings, and process in a boiling water bath for 10 minutes (see page 11).

Let these pickles cure for at least 48 hours before eating.

BASIC PICKLED JALAPEÑO PEPPERS

THESE PICKLED JALAPEÑO PEPPERS ARE UTILITARIAN canning at its best. Pickling without the addition of herbs or a spice mix means that they remain a fiery blank slate, perfect for adding to salsas, taco filling, chili, or scattering atop plates of nachos. I like to put these up in either half- or quarter-pint jars, as I struggle to move through an entire pint in a timely manner, but if your household is more into consuming spicy food, feel free to use the pints. And, if jalapeño peppers aren't your bag, do know that this technique can be used for any small, hot pepper.

MAKES 5 (HALF-PINT/250 ML) JARS

2 cups/480 ml distilled white vinegar
2 tablespoons pickling salt
1 pound/455 g jalapeño peppers, sliced in half lengthwise

Prepare a boiling water bath and 5 half-pint/250 ml jars according to the process on page 10. Place the lids in a small saucepan, cover them with water, and simmer over very low heat.

Combine the vinegar, 2 cups/400 ml water, and salt in a pot over high heat and bring the brine to a boil.

Meanwhile, pack the peppers into the sterilized jars. Slowly pour the hot brine over the peppers in each jar, leaving ½ inch/12 mm headspace. Gently tap the jars on a towel-lined countertop to help loosen any bubbles before using a wooden chopstick to dislodge any remaining bubbles. Check the headspace again and add more brine if necessary.

Wipe the rims, apply the lids and rings, and process in a boiling water bath for 5 minutes (see page 11).

Let these pickles cure for at least 1 week before eating.

Note: Working with hot peppers can be dangerous business. I make a practice of keeping some chemical-resistant gloves around the kitchen to protect my hands from the burn of the oils. If you do end up with burning fingers, I recommend rinsing the area right away with a diluted bleach solution, as it helps alleviate the burn.

PICKLED CARROTS AND DAIKON RADISH COINS

HIS RECIPE IS MY INTERPRETATION OF THE FRESH
pickles often served alongside entrées at Vietnamese restaurants.
After I made them, I discovered that they are equally good tucked
inside a homemade taco or stacked inside a turkey sandwich. I will often find
myself eating these mindlessly from the jar, in those moments while I
ponder the contents of our refrigerator and hope that dinner inspiration will
suddenly strike. If you've never come across daikon radish before, it can
typically be found in the produce section of your local Asian grocery store.

MAKES 3 (1-PINT/500 ML) JARS

1 pound/455 g carrots

1 pound/455 g young daikon radish

$1\frac{1}{2}$ cups/360 ml distilled white vinegar

$\frac{3}{4}$ cup/150 g granulated sugar

3 tablespoons pickling salt

$1\frac{1}{2}$ teaspoons ground ginger

3 tablespoons coriander seeds

2 teaspoons black mustard seeds

$\frac{1}{2}$ teaspoon red pepper flakes

3 whole star anise

Prepare a boiling water bath and 3 regular-mouth 1-pint/500 ml jars according to the process on page 10. Place the lids in a small saucepan, cover them with water, and simmer over very low heat.

Using a mandoline or food processor with the slicing blade, slice the carrots and daikon radish into paper-thin rounds and set aside.

Combine the vinegar, $1\frac{1}{2}$ cups/360 ml water, sugar, salt, and ground ginger in a pot and bring the brine to a boil.

Meanwhile, combine the remaining spices in a small bowl and stir to blend. Add the spice blend to the sterilized jars, distributing evenly.

Once the brine has come to a boil, add the sliced vegetables to the brine in the pot. Stir to combine and remove from the heat.

(continued)

Using tongs, add the vegetables to the jars. Slowly pour the hot brine over the vegetables in each jar, leaving ½ inch/12 mm of headspace. Gently tap the jars on a towel-lined countertop to help loosen any bubbles before using a wooden chopstick to dislodge any remaining bubbles. Check the headspace again and add more brine if necessary.

Wipe the rims, apply the lids and rings, and process in a boiling water bath for 5 minutes (see page 11).

Because they're so thinly sliced, these pickles don't require any curing time and can be eaten immediately.

PICKLED BRUSSELS SPROUTS

BRUSSELS SPROUTS ARE ONE OF THE MORE VERS-atile vegetables out there. Blanched and roasted whole, halved and pan-braised, or shredded and topped with a light dressing, they can easily play a variety of culinary roles. If you haven't done it already, it's time to add "pickled" to the list of Brussels sprouts options. The brine softens them slightly and infuses them with satisfying tartness all the way through.

MAKES 4 (1-PINT/500 ML) JARS

2 cups/480 ml distilled white vinegar
3 tablespoons pickling salt
8 garlic cloves, peeled
2 teaspoons black peppercorns, divided
2 teaspoons coriander seed, divided
1 teaspoon celery seed, divided
1 teaspoon red pepper flakes, divided
1 teaspoon cumin seed, divided
2 pounds/910 g Brussels sprouts, trimmed and sliced in half

Prepare a boiling water bath and 4 regular-mouth 1-pint/500 ml jars according to the process on page 10. Place the lids in a small saucepan, cover them with water, and simmer over very low heat.

Combine the vinegar, 2 cups/480 ml water, and pickling salt in a pot and bring the brine to a boil.

Meanwhile, add 2 garlic cloves, $\frac{1}{2}$ teaspoon peppercorns, $\frac{1}{2}$ teaspoon coriander seed, $\frac{1}{4}$ teaspoon celery seed, $\frac{1}{4}$ teaspoon red pepper flakes, and $\frac{1}{4}$ teaspoon cumin seed to each sterilized jar.

Pack the sprouts into the jars as tightly as you can manage, but without mangling them.

Slowly pour the hot brine over the Brussels sprouts, leaving $\frac{1}{2}$ inch/12 mm headspace. Gently tap the jars on a towel-lined countertop to help loosen any bubbles before using a wooden chopstick to dislodge any remaining bubbles. Check the headspace again and add more brine if necessary.

Wipe the rims, apply the lids and rings, and process in a boiling water bath for 10 minutes (see page 11).

Let these pickles cure for at least 1 week before eating.

Note: If you're working with fresh-from-the-stalk sprouts, there's no need to cut the little ones in half. Just aim to have everything in a generally uniform size as it goes into the jar.

GINGERY PICKLED BEETS

MY MOTHER ADORES BEETS. WHILE SHE WAS PREG-nant with me, she regularly guzzled Manischewitz borscht straight from the jar. I too am an avowed beet lover. This particular pickle was inspired by a recipe for pickled golden beets that Kevin West posted on his beautiful blog, Saving the Season. I will be forever appreciative for his nudge to spike beet brine with a shot of ginger.

MAKES 3 (1-PINT/500 ML) JARS

2 pounds/910 g red beets
2 cups/480 ml apple cider vinegar
2 tablespoons pickling salt
1 cup/200 g sugar
1 cinnamon stick
1 (2-inch/5 cm) piece fresh ginger, peeled and thinly sliced

Scrub the beets, removing the greens and long roots. Place the beets in a pot and cover with water. Simmer over medium heat until the beets are just tender, about 30 to 45 minutes depending on the size of your beets. Drain and rinse with cold water. When the beets are cool enough to handle, rub the skins off with your fingers. (Wear plastic gloves or resealable plastic bags on your hands if you're averse to pink-stained skin.) Trim the unwieldy ends, cut the beets into wedges, and set aside.

Prepare a boiling water bath and 3 regular-mouth 1-pint/500 ml jars according to the process on page 10. Place the lids in a small saucepan, cover them with water, and simmer over very low heat.

Combine the vinegar, 2 cups/480 ml water, salt, sugar, cinnamon stick, and ginger slices in a pot and bring the brine to a boil.

Meanwhile, pack the beet wedges into the sterilized jars. Slowly pour the hot brine over the beets in each jar (making sure to include 2 to 3 ginger slices in each jar), leaving ½ inch/12 mm headspace. Gently tap the jars on a towel-lined countertop to help loosen any bubbles before using a wooden chopstick to dislodge any remaining bubbles. Check the headspace again and add more brine if necessary.

Wipe the rims, apply the lids and rings, and process in a boiling water bath for 10 minutes (see page 11).

Let these pickles cure for at least 1 week before eating.

SWEET-AND-SOUR PICKLED RED ONIONS

IF YOU WERE TO PLOT CONDIMENTS ON A FAMILY TREE, you'd find that these pickled red onions are the wild-child granddaughter of caramelized onion jam and the second cousin of the hot dog relish you find at the ball park. They are sophisticated, a little bit slippery, and equally at home draped across a hamburger or dolloped on a salad of baby arugula.

MAKES 3 (1-PINT/500 ML) JARS

2 cups/480 ml apple cider vinegar

³/₄ cup/150 g granulated sugar

2 tablespoons pickling salt

3 pounds/1.4 kg red onions, trimmed and thinly sliced

2 teaspoons mustard seed

1 teaspoon celery seed

¹/₂ teaspoon red pepper flakes

Prepare a boiling water bath and 3 regular-mouth pint jars according to the process on page 10. Place the lids in a small saucepan, cover them with water, and simmer over very low heat.

Combine the vinegar, 1¹/₂ cups/360 ml water, sugar, and salt in a pot over high heat and bring the brine to a boil.

Add sliced onions to brine and stir to combine. Reduce heat to medium and simmer briefly to soften onions.

Meanwhile, combine the remaining spices in a small bowl and stir to blend. Add the spice blend to the sterilized jars, distributing evenly.

Using tongs, evenly divide the onions between the 3 jars. Pour hot brine into each jar, leaving ¹/₂ inch/12 mm headspace. Gently tap the jars on a towel-lined countertop to help loosen any bubbles before using a wooden chopstick to dislodge any remaining bubbles. Check the headspace again and add more brine if necessary.

Wipe the rims, apply the lids and rings, and process in a boiling water bath for 10 minutes (see page 11).

Let these pickles cure for at least 48 hours before eating.

PICKLED GREEN TOMATOES

GARDENERS NEVER KNOW WHETHER THEY'LL HAVE a bumper crop of ripe tomatoes or gallons of green tomatoes issuing forth from their plants. This recipe transforms what could be a massive disappointment into something tasty.

MAKES 3 (1-PINT/500 ML) JARS

1 cup/240 ml distilled white vinegar
1 tablespoon pickling salt
6 garlic cloves, peeled
3 teaspoons dill seed, divided
$3/4$ teaspoon peppercorns, divided
3 bay leaves
2 pounds/910 g green tomatoes,
　　stemmed and cut into wedges

Prepare a boiling water bath and 3 regular-mouth 1-pint/500 ml jars according to the process on page 10. the process on page 000. Place the lids in a small saucepan, cover them with water, and simmer over very low heat.

Combine the vinegar, 1 cup/240 ml water, and the pickling salt in a pot and bring the brine to a boil.

Meanwhile, add 2 garlic cloves, 1 teaspoon dill seed, $1/4$ teaspoon peppercorns, and 1 bay leaf to each sterilized jar. Pack the tomato wedges into the jars as tightly as you can manage, while trying not to mangle them.

Slowly pour the hot brine over the tomatoes in each jar, leaving $1/2$ inch/12 mm headspace. Gently tap the jars on a towel-lined countertop to help loosen any bubbles before using a wooden chopstick to dislodge any remaining bubbles. Check the headspace again and add more brine if necessary.

Wipe the rims, apply the lids and rings, and process in a boiling water bath for 10 minutes (see page 11).

Let these pickles cure for at least 1 week before eating.

LEMONY PICKLED CAULIFLOWER

WHEN I FIRST BEGAN TO MOVE BEYOND BASIC cucumber pickles, my friend Val made a plaintive request for pickled cauliflower. These crunchy, lemon-infused cauliflower florets are so, so satisfying in salads or with fruity oil, bread, and cheese.

MAKES 3 (1-PINT/500 ML) JARS

2 cups/480 ml distilled white vinegar

3 tablespoons pickling salt

1 lemon, sliced

1 $\frac{1}{2}$ teaspoons mustard seed, divided

1 $\frac{1}{2}$ teaspoons cumin seed, divided

$\frac{3}{4}$ teaspoon red pepper flakes, divided

$\frac{3}{4}$ teaspoon black peppercorns, divided

1 head cauliflower, cut into small florets
  (1 $\frac{1}{2}$ to 2 pounds/455 to 680 g)

Prepare a boiling water bath and 3 regular-mouth 1-pint/500 ml jars according to the process on page 10. Place the lids in a small saucepan, cover them with water, and simmer over very low heat.

Combine the vinegar, 1 $\frac{1}{2}$ cups/360 ml water, and pickling salt and bring the brine to a boil. Meanwhile, place a lemon slice at the bottom of each sterilized jar. Add $\frac{1}{2}$ teaspoon mustard seed, $\frac{1}{2}$ teaspoon cumin seed, $\frac{1}{4}$ teaspoon red pepper flakes, and $\frac{1}{4}$ teaspoon peppercorns to each jar.

Pack the florets into the jars tightly, but without mangling them. Slowly pour the hot brine over the cauliflower in each jar, leaving $\frac{1}{2}$ inch/12 mm headspace. Gently tap the jars on a towel-lined countertop to help loosen any bubbles before using a wooden chopstick to dislodge any remaining bubbles. Check the headspace again and add more brine if necessary. Top each jar with another slice of lemon.

Wipe the rims, apply the lids and rings, and process in a boiling water bath for 10 minutes (see page11).

Let these pickles cure for at least 1 week before eating.

SPICED PICKLED PEAR HALVES

I **THINK PEARS WERE MEANT FOR PICKLING. WHILE** they have a perfectly nice taste on their own, they are also mellow enough to happily absorb a world of flavors. I like these pickled pears cut into thin slices and heaped atop a salad of baby lettuces. They play well with goat cheese. And should you be able to manage it, save a jar for the holidays. I don't peel my pears before pickling, and don't find it necessary. However, if you're partial to a peeled pear, feel free to do so.

MAKES 4 (1-PINT/500 ML) JARS

2 cups/480 ml distilled white vinegar
1 cup/200 g granulated sugar
$\frac{1}{2}$ cup/120 ml honey
1 (2-inch/5 cm) piece fresh ginger, sliced into thin coins
4 thin lemon slices
4 cinnamon sticks
1 teaspoon whole cloves, divided
2 pounds/910 g firm pears (like Bartlett or Anjou)

Prepare a boiling water bath and 4 regular-mouth 1-pint/500 ml jars according to the process on page 10. Place the lids in a small saucepan, cover them with water, and simmer over very low heat.

Combine the vinegar, 2 cups/480 ml water, the sugar, and honey in a pot and bring to a boil. Meanwhile, cut the pears in half and use a melon baller to remove the cores.

Divide the ginger among the jars. Add 1 lemon slice, 1 cinnamon stick, and $\frac{1}{4}$ teaspoon cloves to each jar. Pack the pear halves into the jars tightly without squashing them.

Slowly pour the hot brine over the pears in each jar, leaving $\frac{1}{2}$ inch/12 mm of headspace. Gently tap the jars on a towel-lined countertop to help loosen any bubbles before using a wooden chopstick to dislodge any remaining bubbles. Check the headspace again and add more brine if necessary.

Wipe the rims, apply the lids and rings, and process in a hot water bath for 10 minutes (see page 11).

Allow at least 1 week of curing time before opening these pickles to taste them.

PICKLED SWEET CHERRIES

WHEN MY FRIEND SHAY FIRST TASTED THESE pickled cherries, she looked at me in disbelief and said, "Cherry pie!" And she was right. The sweet brine performs some sort of miracle on your taste buds so that your brain receives the flavors of a perfectly balanced pie. They pair up nicely with a creamy cheese and also make for a delicious snack straight out of the jar.

MAKES 4 (1-PINT/500 ML) JARS

$2\frac{1}{2}$ cups/600 ml distilled white vinegar

2 cups/400 g granulated sugar

2 tablespoons pickling salt

4 bay leaves

32 black peppercorns

$2\frac{1}{2}$ pounds/1.2 kg sweet cherries,
   washed with stems trimmed (see note)

Prepare a boiling water bath and 4 regular-mouth (1-pint/500 ml) jars according to the process on page 10. Place the lids in a small saucepan, cover them with water, and simmer over very low heat.

Combine the vinegar, 2 cups/480 ml water, the sugar, and pickling salt in a pot and bring the brine to a boil.

Meanwhile, place 1 bay leaf and 8 peppercorns in each sterilized jar. Pack the cherries into the jars as tightly as you can manage, while trying not to squash them.

Slowly pour the hot brine over the cherries in each jar, leaving $\frac{1}{2}$ inch/12 mm of headspace. Gently tap the jars on a towel-lined countertop to help loosen any bubbles before using a wooden chopstick to dislodge any remaining bubbles. Check the headspace again and add more brine if necessary.

Wipe the rims, apply the lids and rings, and process in a boiling water bath for 10 minutes (see page 11).

Let pickles cure for at least 48 hours before eating.

Note: I like to leave the stems on the cherries when pickling them because they help them better retain their shape. I do suggest you trim all the stems to a uniform length of about 1 inch, as it makes for a nicer presentation.

SALSAS & RELISHES

I WAS A TEENAGER WHEN I FIRST LEARNED THAT SALSA was something one could make at home. Up until that point, I functioned under the belief that salsa was the product of some mysterious alchemy, something that could only be purchased at Safeway or Trader Joe's. This culinary revelation came when my parents went on a trip to Europe leaving my sister and me with a family friend.

Deliah had a completely different approach to food than the three balanced meals a day routine that Raina and I were familiar with. She used lots of bright, vivid flavors and believed that dinner could consist of fresh salsa, tortilla chips, and a dollop of sour cream. Needless to say, we adored her.

One afternoon, I watched as she made the salsa. She dragged a colander of tomatoes out to the living room coffee table, along with onions, garlic, cilantro, a single hot pepper, a cutting board, mixing bowl, sharp knife, and salt shaker. She set up her tools in front of the TV and chopped while watching Oprah. When everything was combined, she set the bowl aside for an hour, to let the flavors mingle. Later, we feasted until our lips blistered from the acids.

Later, I taught my mom how to make salsa and we would make batch after batch from the tomatoes that grew in the backyard, using it to top scrambled eggs or digging into with chips. The first year I was living in Philadelphia, my dad and sister came to visit me for Thanksgiving. My mom couldn't fly that year, so in her place, she sent a quart jar of homemade salsa in her place, triple wrapped and tucked into my dad's checked luggage. It wasn't quite as good as seeing her, but nearly.

These days, fresh salsa is one of my summertime refrigerator staples. However, because its time is so fleeting, I also make up at least a dozen jars of various, shelf-stable salsas and relishes, to tide me over until the summer season returns.

One thing to note about these recipes is that they read like a ton of work. However, it's really just all chopping. Once the knife work is done, it's just a matter of simmering, filling the jars, and processing. I recommend inviting a friend over to help make the work go faster.

CHUNKY TOMATILLO SALSA

TOMATILLOS RANGE IN SIZE, THOUGH THE ONES YOU find at grocery stores are typically the size of an apricot, and are covered by a papery husk. When you pull the husk back, they look like small, green tomatoes and are covered by a sticky substance. Once they are husked and washed, they are ready for chopping and cooking. This salsa is terrific as a dipping sauce, and can also be used in chile verde or green posole.

MAKES 3 (1-PINT/500 ML) JARS

4 pounds/1.8 kg tomatillos, husked, washed, and finely chopped
1 cup/160 g finely chopped onion (about 1 medium onion)
3 to 4 jalapeño peppers, minced (seeds removed for a milder salsa)
8 garlic cloves, minced
1 tablespoon ground cumin
2 teaspoons sea salt
$\frac{1}{2}$ cup/120 ml bottled lime juice
$\frac{1}{4}$ cup/4 g minced fresh cilantro

Prepare a boiling water bath and 3 regular-mouth 1-pint/500 ml jars according to the process on page 10. Place the lids in a small saucepan, cover them with water, and simmer over very low heat.

Combine the tomatillos, onion, jalapeños, and garlic in a large pot. Bring to a boil, then reduce the heat and simmer 10 minutes. Add the cumin, sea salt, lime juice, and cilantro. If you prefer a smoother salsa, you can use an immersion blender to break down some of the salsa at this time.

Cook for an additional 10 minutes. Taste the salsa and add more salt, cumin, or lime juice if necessary.

Ladle the hot salsa into the prepared jars, leaving $\frac{1}{2}$ inch/12 mm of headspace. Wipe the rims, apply the lids and rings, and process in a boiling water bath for 15 minutes (see page 11).

When the processing time is up, remove the canning pot from the heat and remove the lid. Let the jars sit in the pot for an additional 5 minutes. This helps to prevent the salsa from reacting to the rapid temperature change and bubbling out of the jars.

BASIC TOMATO SALSA

I FREQUENTLY HAVE TO TELL PEOPLE THAT THEY CAN'T just put their beloved fresh salsa recipe in a jar and preserve it. Because salsa contains so many low-acid ingredients, you've got to balance them out with plenty of acid to ensure a safe product. I offer up this salsa recipe as balm to that particular disappointment. Though it's cooked, this salsa retains some of the same bright, fiery flavors and is miles better than any cooked salsa you'll find on your grocery store shelves.

MAKES 4 (1-PINT/500 ML) JARS

6 cups chopped Roma or paste tomatoes
 (about 3 pounds/1.4 kg tomatoes)
2 cups/320 g chopped yellow onion (about 2 medium onions)
1 cup/150 g chopped red bell pepper (1 large pepper)
$1^3/4$ cups/420 ml cider vinegar
$1/4$ cup/50 g granulated sugar
3 jalapeño peppers, minced
4 garlic cloves, minced
2 tablespoons bottled lime juice
1 tablespoon sea salt
1 cup/16 g chopped fresh cilantro

Prepare a boiling water bath and 4 regular-mouth 1-pint/500 ml jars according to the process on page 10. Place the lids in a small saucepan, cover them with water, and simmer over very low heat.

Combine the tomatoes, onion, chopped red pepper, vinegar, sugar, jalapeños, garlic, lime juice, and salt in a large pot. Bring to a boil, then reduce the heat and simmer for 10 minutes or until the salsa no longer looks watery. Stir in the chopped cilantro.

Taste and add additional jalapeño, lime juice, or salt if necessary.

Ladle the hot salsa into the prepared jars, leaving $1/2$ inch/12 mm of headspace. Wipe the rims, apply the lids and rings, and process in a boiling water bath for 15 minutes (see page 11).

When the processing time is up, remove the canning pot from the heat and remove the lid. Let the jars sit in the pot for an additional 5 minutes. This helps to prevent the salsa from reacting to the rapid temperature change and bubbling out of the jars.

ROASTED CORN SALSA ∽

TRADER JOE'S SELLS A SALSA THAT MY PARENTS are positively addicted to. Made of sweet corn, red peppers, and spiked with plenty of coriander, it's a dream folded into a burrito or heaped on a pile of oven-toasted nachos. Though I think it's a tasty enough product, I couldn't resist the urge to devise my own version. Charring the corn gives it a smoky flavor that is irresistible.

MAKES 4 (1-PINT/500 ML) JARS

8 ears fresh corn, shucked with silks removed

5 cups chopped tomatoes (approximately
   3 pounds/1.4 kg tomatoes)

1 cup/150 g chopped poblano peppers (about 2 large peppers)

1 cup/160 g chopped red onion (1 small onion)

1 1/2 cups/360 ml apple cider vinegar

1/4 cup/60 ml bottled lime juice

2/3 cup/130 g granulated sugar

1 1/2 teaspoons ground cumin

1/2 teaspoon red pepper flakes

1 teaspoon sea salt

1 teaspoon coriander seed

Prepare a boiling water bath and 4 regular-mouth 1-pint/500 ml jars according to the process on page 10. Place the lids in a small saucepan, cover them with water, and simmer over very low heat.

Preheat the broiler to high. Place the corn on a rimmed baking sheet and place under the broiler. Broil the corn, turning, until the kernels are lightly browned on all sides, about 3 to 5 minutes for each side. If you prefer, this roasting can also be done outside on a grill.

When the corn is cool enough to handle, cut the kernels from the cobs with a large, sharp knife. (You should have approximately 3 cups/460 g corn kernels.)

Combine the corn kernels, tomatoes, peppers, onion, vinegar, lime juice, sugar, cumin, red pepper flakes, salt, and coriander in a large pot and bring to a boil. Reduce the heat and simmer for 10 minutes, until the liquid has reduced. Taste and adjust the spices as needed.

Ladle the hot salsa into the prepared jars, leaving $\frac{1}{2}$ inch/12 mm of headspace. Wipe the rims, apply the lids and rings, and process in a boiling water bath for 15 minutes (see page 11).

When the processing time is up, remove the canning pot from the heat and remove the lid. Let the jars sit in the pot for an additional 5 minutes. This helps to prevent the salsa from reacting to the rapid temperature change and bubbling out of the jars.

PEACH SALSA

I **F YOU'RE A FAN OF FRUITY SALSAS, THIS IS AN EXCEL-** lent one to try. It essentially substitutes peaches for the traditional tomato, while keeping the rest of the standard ingredients intact. I can gobble down an entire pint with tortilla chips if given the chance. I also like to use a jar as a simmer sauce for chicken legs and thighs.

MAKES 4 (1-PINT/500 ML) JARS

6 cups peeled, pitted, and chopped peaches
  (about 4 pounds/1.8 kg)
1 ½ cups/240 g chopped red onion (about 1 large onion)
1 ½ cups/300 ml distilled white vinegar
1 cup/150 g chopped red bell pepper (about 1 large pepper)
¾ cup/150 g granulated sugar
3 jalapeño peppers, minced
3 garlic cloves, minced
1 teaspoon ground cumin
¼ teaspoon cayenne pepper

Prepare a boiling water bath and 4 regular-mouth 1-pint/500 ml jars according to the process on page 10. Place the lids in a small saucepan, cover them with water, and simmer over very low heat.

Combine the peaches, onion, vinegar, chopped red pepper, sugar, jalapeños, garlic, cumin, and cayenne in a large pot. Bring to a boil, then reduce the heat and simmer for 10 minutes, until the salsa no longer looks watery. Taste and add additional jalapeño or vinegar, if necessary.

Ladle the hot salsa into the prepared jars, leaving ½ inch/12 mm of headspace. Wipe the rims, apply the lids and rings, and process in a boiling water bath for 15 minutes (see page 11).

When the processing time is up, remove the canning pot from the heat and remove the lid. Let the jars sit in the pot for an additional 5 minutes. This helps to prevent the salsa from reacting to the rapid temperature change and bubbling out of the jars.

ZUCCHINI AND PEPPER RELISH

LOVE A GOOD STADIUM HOT DOG. TO ME, THE PERFECT dog is served in a squishy bun and dressed with mustard, relish, and chopped onions (dispensed in bulk from a stainless steel container with a rotary handle that controls the output). This relish tastes just like my memory of that stadium stuff, only I know everything that went into it. Plus, it uses up piles of produce, which is a huge plus in July or August.

MAKES 5 (1-PINT/500 ML) JARS

6 cups/890 g chopped green bell pepper (about 8 whole peppers)

6 cups grated zucchini (about 3 pounds zucchini)

$2\frac{1}{2}$ cups grated onion (about 2 large onions)

4 cups/960 ml apple cider vinegar, divided

2 cups/400 g granulated sugar

2 tablespoons sea salt

2 tablespoons mustard seed

1 teaspoon celery seed

$\frac{1}{2}$ teaspoon red pepper flakes

Prepare a boiling water bath and 5 regular-mouth 1-pint/500 ml jars according to the process on page 10. Place the lids in a small saucepan, cover them with water, and simmer over very low heat.

Combine the chopped bell pepper, zucchini, and onion in a large, nonreactive pot. Stir in 2 cups/480 ml of the apple cider vinegar and bring to a simmer over medium heat. Cook until the vegetables have cooked down, about 30 minutes.

Drain the vegetables and return to the pot. Add the remaining apple cider vinegar, sugar, salt, mustard seed, celery seed, and red pepper flakes. Bring to a simmer and cook for 5 minutes.

Ladle the relish into the prepared jars, leaving $\frac{1}{2}$ inch/12 mm of headspace. Gently tap the jars on a towel-lined countertop to help loosen any bubbles before using a wooden chopstick to dislodge any remaining bubbles. Wipe the rims, apply the lids and rings, and process in a boiling water bath for 10 minutes (see page 11).

(continued)

When the processing time is up, remove the canning pot from the heat and remove the lid. Let the jars sit in the pot for an additional 5 minutes. This helps to prevent the relish from reacting to the rapid temperature change and bubbling out of the jars.

CARAMELIZED RED ONION RELISH

IF YOU LIKE CARAMELIZED ONIONS, YOU MUST TRY this relish. It is sweet (but not saccharine), substantive, and smooth. I like to eat it with a creamy goat cheese or freshly made ricotta. It's also great on pizza in place of the tomato sauce. Once you have this one on your pantry shelf, you'll soon find that you'll be putting it on everything. And I don't think there's anything wrong with that.

MAKES 3 (1-PINT/500 ML) JARS

1 tablespoon unsalted butter

4 to 5 large red onions, sliced into thin half-moons (about 10 cups/1.2 kg)

1 cup/200 g (packed) brown sugar

1 cup/240 ml apple cider vinegar

1/2 cup/120 ml malt vinegar

2 teaspoons sea salt

1 teaspoon garlic powder

1/2 teaspoon freshly ground black pepper

1/4 teaspoon cayenne pepper

Prepare a boiling water bath and 3 regular-mouth 1-pint/500 ml jars according to the process on page 10. Place the lids in a small saucepan, cover them with water, and simmer over very low heat.

Melt the butter over medium-low heat in a large, nonreactive and add the onions. Cook until the onions are golden and fragrant, about 20 to 25 minutes.

Add the remaining ingredients. Increase the heat and bring to a boil, then reduce the heat and simmer for 10 minutes, until the liquid has reduced.

Ladle the relish into the prepared jars. Gently tap the jars on a towel-lined counter-top to help loosen any bubbles before using a wooden chopstick to dislodge any remaining bubbles. Wipe the rims, apply the lids and rings, and process in a boiling water bath for 15 minutes (see page 11).

When the processing time is up, remove the canning pot from the heat and remove the lid. Let the jars sit in the pot for an additional 5 minutes. This helps to prevent the relish from reacting to the rapid temperature change and bubbling out of the jars.

TOMATOES

FOR MY FIRST FIFTEEN YEARS OF LIFE, ANY CONtact with raw tomatoes made me break out in an itchy, red rash. This was a hard thing in a household of tomato fans, particularly during the months of July, August, and September, when our backyard plants were growing prodigiously and all my mom wanted to make for dinner were salads of cucumber and sliced ripe tomato. I was also wary of cooked tomatoes and would only eat pasta sauces that were puréed smooth. It was a pain for everyone involved.

Thankfully, around the time I turned sixteen, the allergy disappeared and I discovered just why people raved about homegrown tomatoes. They are amazing. Since then, I've spent my summers making up for those lost years. I eat them with every meal where they make sense and I typically can up to a hundred pounds of locally grown paste or Roma tomatoes every September (always praising my body for having the smarts to outgrow that allergy). My goal is to put up enough local tomatoes to ensure that I won't run out until May or June.

Most years, the bulk of my tomato preservation is done in quarts of whole, peeled tomatoes. I find them to be the most versatile when it comes to cooking (and, when you're trying to move a hundred pounds of tomatoes through your kitchen in a three-day weekend, a single, streamlined process is your friend). If I'm not in too much of a rush, I also make a basic tomato sauce (truly, no more than a smooth, basil-spiked version of the whole peeled tomatoes), a marinara/pizza sauce (for those nights when you need something that's a little closer to being ready to eat than a jar of whole tomatoes), and a couple variations on chopped tomatoes.

Anytime you talk about canning tomatoes, the issue of acid content must be considered. We all think of tomatoes as being incredibly high in acid, right? But when it comes to having enough acid for boiling water bath canning, tomatoes are actually in the grey zone. Plums and apples have more acid than a basic tomato does. This means that tomato products have to have acid added to them to be safe for canning. You may be thinking, "But my grandma never added acid to her tomatoes and we were always fine." There's a good reason for that. Modern tomatoes have been bred to be sweeter and lower in acid. Nice for today's palate, but not so good for canning safety. It's easy enough to remedy the acid situation when it comes to canning by adding lemon juice to your products before canning. Make sure you don't skip or reduce the amount of acid in the following recipes, as it a key player in ensuring the safety of your finished products.

WHOLE PEELED TOMATOES

THESE TOMATOES ARE ONE OF MY PANTRY STAPLES and after several years of canning them at home, I find it hard to remember how I lived without them. Once you find your rhythm, the process of removing the cores, scoring the end to make peeling easy, and blanching the tomatoes briefly in a pot of boiling water they go fairly fast. Try them in soups, stews, or crushed over a pizza crust (a particularly good technique when I've used up all the marinara sauce). I like to can these in quart jars and so those are the instructions given below. If you feel that pints would be more appropriate for you, feel free to use pint (500 ml) jars and reduce the processing time to 40 minutes.

MAKES 4 (1-QUART/1 LITER) JARS

10 pounds/4.5 kg Roma or paste tomatoes
$\frac{1}{2}$ cup/120 ml bottled lemon juice, divided

Prepare a boiling water bath and 4 regular-mouth 1-quart/1 liter jars according to the process on page 10. Place the lids in a small saucepan, cover them with water, and simmer over very low heat.

Bring a large pot of water to a boil. While it heats, core the tomatoes and, using a small, sharp knife, score the bottom of each tomato with a shallow X. Fill a large bowl two-thirds full with ice-cold water. (The cold water stops the cooking and cools the tomatoes down enough for you to peel them after blanching.)

Working in batches, add the tomatoes to the boiling water and cook for 1 to 2 minutes. Immediately transfer the tomatoes to the bowl of ice-cold water to cool. Once they tomatoes are cool, remove them from the cold water bath. Repeat with the remaining tomatoes, making sure to give the water a chance to come back up to boiling between batches. If the water isn't hot enough, you will have a hard time removing the skins during peeling.

When the blanched tomatoes are cool enough to handle, grab one and peel the skin off with your fingers. The blanching should have loosened it to the point where it curls off the tomato and is easy to pull free.

Bring a full kettle of drinkable water to a boil. This will be the liquid you add to your tomatoes.

(continued)

Add 2 tablespoons bottled lemon juice to each prepared jar. Gently pack the peeled tomatoes into the jars, taking care not to mash or mangle them too badly. They should retain their general tomato form. I find that I can get 5 to 6 average-sized Roma tomatoes into a quart jar.

Pour the boiling water over the tomatoes in each jar, leaving $1/2$ inch/12 mm of headspace. Gently tap the jars on a towel-lined countertop to help loosen any bubbles before using a wooden chopstick to dislodge any remaining bubbles. Check the headspace again and add more boiling water if necessary.

Wipe the rims, apply the lids and rings, and process in a boiling water bath for 45 minutes (see page 11).

Note: When it comes to choosing tomatoes for canning, I find that either paste tomatoes (varieties developed for their meatiness and lack of liquid) or Roma tomatoes are best for canning. I like plum tomatoes, but they tend to be smaller than the Romas or paste tomatoes, which means more coring and peeling work. I've found that it's best to avoid heirloom tomatoes, as they're far juicier and harder to work with.

CHOPPED TOMATOES

HAD MY MOM BEEN THE TYPE TO CAN HER OWN TOM-atoes (she is strictly a jam and applesauce canner), these would have been her tomatoes of choice. Roughly chopped and simmered a bit to help thicken their juices, these are great in soups, stews, and those one-skillet meals that so many of us fall back on for fast and tasty nourishment. My one-skillet go-to starts with chopped onion and garlic and ends with cubed zucchini, a pound of browned ground beef, and some of these chopped tomatoes.

MAKES 4 (1-PINT/500 ML) JARS

6 pounds/2.7 kg Roma or paste tomatoes
$1/4$ cup/60 ml bottled lemon juice, divided

Prepare a boiling water bath and 4 regular-mouth 1-pint/500 ml jars according to the process on page 10. Place the lids in a small saucepan, cover them with water, and simmer over very low heat.

Bring a large pot of water to a boil. While it heats, core the tomatoes and, using a small, sharp knife, score the bottom of each tomato with a shallow X. Fill a large bowl two-thirds full with ice-cold water. (The cold water stops the cooking and cools the tomatoes down enough for you to peel them after blanching.)

Working in batches, add the tomatoes to the boiling water and cook for 1 to 2 minutes. Immediately transfer the tomatoes to the bowl of ice-cold water to cool. Repeat with remaining tomatoes, making sure to give the water a chance to come back up to boiling between batches. If the water isn't hot enough, you will have a hard time removing the skins during peeling.

When the blanched tomatoes are cool enough to handle, grab one and peel the skin off with your fingers. The blanching should have loosened it to the point where it curls off the tomato and is easy to pull free.

Chop the peeled tomatoes and place them in a pot with as much of the juices as you're able to capture during the chopping process. Bring them to a boil, then reduce the heat and simmer 30-35 minutes, until the juices thicken. Stir regularly to prevent burning.

Add 1 tablespoon of bottled lemon juice to each prepared jar. Ladle the hot chopped tomatoes with their juices into the jars, leaving $1/2$ inch/12 mm of headspace. Gently tap the jars on a towel-lined countertop to help loosen any bubbles before using a wooden chopstick to dislodge any remaining bubbles and add additional tomatoes, if necessary.

Wipe the rims, apply the lids and rings, and process in a boiling water bath for 35 minutes (see page 11).

Note: It's a best canning practice to use bottled lemon juice when you're adding the juice for its role as an acidifier. This is because bottled lemon juice has a dependable acidity level. However, when you are adding lemon juice for flavor (as in the jam recipes earlier in the book) fresh squeezed is preferred.

ROTEL-STYLE TOMATOES

FITTINGLY, IT WAS A FRIEND FROM TEXAS WHO introduced me to Rotel tomatoes. They are fairly basic chopped and canned tomatoes that have been souped up with the addition of hot peppers. I confess that once a year, I set aside my commitments to eating unprocessed foods and melt a hunk of American cheese with a jar of these tomatoes in order to create queso dip. Healthy? Not so much. But it's oh, so good.

MAKES 2 (1-PINT/500 ML) JARS

4 pounds/1.8 kg Roma or paste tomatoes
9 jalapeño peppers, diced
3 tablespoons bottled lemon juice, divided

Prepare a boiling water bath and 2 regular-mouth 1-pint/500 ml jars according to the process on page 10. Place the lids in a small saucepan, cover them with water, and simmer over very low heat.

Bring a large pot of water to a boil. While it heats, core the tomatoes and, using a small, sharp knife, score the bottom of each tomato with a shallow X. Fill a large bowl two-thirds full with ice-cold water. (The cold water stops the cooking and cools the tomatoes down enough for you to peel them after blanching.)

Working in batches, add the tomatoes to the boiling water and cook for 1 to 2 minutes. Transfer the tomatoes to the bowl of ice-cold water to cool. Repeat with remaining tomatoes, making sure to give the water a chance to come back up to boiling between batches. If the water isn't hot enough, you will have a hard time removing the skins during peeling.

When the blanched tomatoes are cool enough to handle, grab one and peel the skin off with your fingers. The blanching should have loosened it to the point where it curls off the tomato and is easy to pull free.

Chop the peeled tomatoes and place them in a pot with as much of the juice as you're able to capture during the chopping process. Add the chopped jalapeños (remember, the more seeds, the hotter the finished product) and bring to a boil. Reduce the heat and simmer until the juices thicken a bit, stirring regularly to prevent burning.

Add 1$\frac{1}{2}$ tablespoons of bottled lemon juice to each prepared jar. Ladle the hot chopped tomatoes with their juices into the jars, leaving $\frac{1}{2}$ inch/12 mm of head-space. Gently tap the jars on a towel-lined countertop to help loosen any bubbles before using a wooden chopstick to dislodge any remaining bubbles and add additional tomatoes, if necessary.

Wipe the rims, apply the lids and rings, and process in a boiling water bath for 35 minutes (see page 11).

BASIC TOMATO SAUCE

THIS SAUCE IS THE PERFECT TOMATO BLANK SLATE. I often tip a jar into a pot of stew when I need a little extra acid and oomph but don't want the texture of whole or chopped tomatoes. Pour this sauce into a pan, add a bit of sautéed garlic and onion, a splash of cream, and a little simmer time, and it quickly becomes tomato soup. You can tuck a basil leaf into each jar just before processing if you want to boost the flavor or you can leave it as is. I like to can this product in pints as opposed to quarts as I feel like that gives me more flexibility. However, if you prefer quarts (or liters) of basic sauce, just increase the processing time to 40 minutes.

MAKES 4 (1-PINT/500 ML) JARS

8 pounds/3.6 kg Roma or paste tomatoes
1 teaspoon salt
$\frac{1}{4}$ cup/60 ml bottled lemon juice, divided
4 basil leaves (optional)

Prepare a boiling water bath and 4 regular-mouth 1-pint/500 ml jars according to the process on page 10. Place the lids in a small saucepan, cover them with water, and simmer over very low heat.

Wash the tomatoes, remove the stems, and cut away any bruises. Chop the first 4 to 5 tomatoes, put them in a pot and bring to a vigorous boil while crushing them with a wooden spoon. Keep the pot at a rapid boil while chopping, adding, and crushing the remaining tomatoes. (This method helps prevent the tomatoes from separating once in the jars. If available, have a friend or family member help you crush and stir while you chop and add). Once all the tomatoes are in the pot, boil for 5 more minutes.

Position a sieve or food mill over a large bowl and press the hot tomatoes through it in batches. Discard the seeds and skins in the sieve and return the sauce to the pot and simmer for 40-50 minutes, until it is reduced by a third.

Add 1 tablespoon of bottled lemon juice to each prepared jar. Pour the hot tomato sauce into the jars, leaving $1/2$-inch/12 mm of headspace. If you're adding a basil leaf to each jar, tuck it in now.

Wipe the rims, apply the lids and rings, and process in a boiling water bath for 35 minutes (see page 11).

MARINARA SAUCE

THIS SAUCE, ADAPTED FROM THE *BALL BLUE BOOK* *of Preserving*, is what I use on pizzas or as the base for larger batches of vegetable-packed pasta sauces. I've also found that it's just the thing for kids who prefer their noodles with just a hint of tomato. When you make this, please stick to the recipe and resist the urge to add extra alliums, which is anything in the onion and garlic family. This is always a struggle for me, since I typically operate under the belief that if a little garlic is good, a whole lot more is even better. As tasty as they are, they are low in acid and so need to be kept in check for the sauce to be safe for boiling water bath canning.

MAKES 4 (1-PINT/500 ML) JARS

1 teaspoon olive oil
$1/2$ cup/80 g chopped yellow onion
3 garlic cloves, finely chopped
1 teaspoon salt
9 pounds/4 kg Roma or paste tomatoes
2 tablespoons finely chopped fresh basil

2 tablespoons finely chopped fresh flat-leaf parsley
6 tablespoons bottled lemon juice, divided

Prepare a boiling water bath and 4 regular-mouth 1-pint/500 ml jars according to the process on page 10. Place the lids in a small saucepan, cover them with water, and simmer over very low heat.

Heat the oil in a large pot over high heat. Add the onion, garlic, and salt and sauté until the onion is translucent, about 5-6 minutes.

While the onions and garlic cook, core and chop the tomatoes. When the onions are translucent, add the chopped tomatoes with any juices. Increase the heat and bring to a boil. Reduce the heat and simmer for 15 to 20 minutes, until the tomatoes have broken down.

Position a sieve or food mill over a large bowl and press the hot tomato mixture through it in batches. Discard the seeds and skins in the sieve and return the sauce to the pot. Stir in the basil and parsley. Simmer the sauce until it is reduced by one-third to one-half, about 40-50 minutes.

Add $1\frac{1}{2}$ tablespoons of bottled lemon juice to each prepared jar. Pour the hot tomato sauce into the jars, leaving $\frac{1}{2}$ inch/12 mm of headspace.

Wipe the rims, apply the lids and rings, and process in a boiling water bath for 35 minutes (see page 11).

SYRUPS

WHEN I WAS IN ELEMENTARY SCHOOL, ESPRESSO culture hit the Pacific Northwest. Suddenly coffee shops, cafés, and drive-thru coffee shacks were everywhere. At that point, my parents still believed that I was too young to be drinking coffee and so said no to my repeated requests for iced lattes and mochas. However, once in a while they'd relent and let me order the only kid-friendly alternative, the Italian soda. I thought it was the height of sophistication. In actuality, it was nothing more than sparkling water with a shot of highly sweetened syrup stirred in.

Though I eventually became a coffee drinker, I'm still a big fan of the Italian soda concept. I make mine at home these days with sparkling water from my seltzer maker (I love this thing—it is so much better than hauling bottles of sparkling water up to my apartment from the grocery store) and a bit of home-made fruit syrup.

But even if you're not a fan of slightly sweet sparking water, don't assume that you should skip this section. Homemade syrups can do more than sweeten beverages. For example, you can whisk the Blueberry-Lemon Syrup into a basic vinaigrette for a sweet-tart salad dressing. The Rhubarb Syrup makes an excellent glaze for cakes, muffins, and scones. Stir a bit of corn-starch into the strawberry syrup and heat for a tasty pancake syrup. If you've had a hard day, stir the cranberry syrup together with some vodka and a bit of sparkling water; as a canner, I get the maximum satisfaction when I serve it over ice in a wide-mouth pint jar.

STRAWBERRY SYRUP

TRADER JOE'S HAS PLAYED A SIGNIFICANT ROLE in my life. In recent years, the specialty grocery has expanded across the country, but when I was a kid it was still just a regional chain local to California. We had one two blocks from our house. I grew up on their peanut butter-filled pretzels, juices, and popsicles. When my family moved to Oregon in 1988, one of the hardest things was leaving Trader Joe's behind. Twice a year, my dad would drive to visit family in the L.A. area and would fill the car with Trader Joe's products for the return trip. Of all the goodies he'd bring back, it was the Sir Strawberry juice that I looked forward to the most. This strawberry syrup reminds me so much of Sir Strawberry.

MAKES 4 (HALF-PINT/250 ML) JARS

2 pints/715 g strawberries, hulled and chopped
2 cups/400 g granulated sugar

Prepare a boiling water bath and 4 half-pint/250 ml jars according to the process on page 10. Place the lids in a small saucepan, cover them with water, and simmer over very low heat.

Combine the strawberries with 3 cups/720 ml water in a medium pot and bring to a boil. Reduce the heat and simmer until the strawberries are soft and have given most of their color to the liquid, about 15 minutes.

Place a large fine-mesh sieve over a large bowl and strain the berries and their juice through the sieve. Let the berries drip undisturbed. Do your best to resist the urge to press the strawberry bits as this will result in a cloudy syrup.

Discard the solids in the sieve and return the strained juice to the pot. Add the sugar and bring to a boil, skimming any foam that appears on the top.

Remove the pot from the heat and pour the hot syrup into the prepared jars, leaving $\frac{1}{2}$ inch/12 mm of headspace. Wipe the rims, apply the lids and rings, and process in a boiling water bath for 10 minutes (see page 11).

RHUBARB SYRUP

AFTER YOU'VE MADE THE VANILLA-RHUBARB JAM (page 22), the Rhubarb Jelly (page 68), and the Rhubarb Chutney (page 103), make sure to take this syrup for a spin. It is a vivid pink and brightly tangy on the tongue. Add a splash to a flute of Prosecco or drizzle a bit over cut melon to brighten the flavors.

MAKES 4 (HALF-PINT/250 ML) JARS

1 $\frac{1}{2}$ pounds/680 g rhubarb stalks, coarsely chopped
2 $\frac{1}{2}$ cups/500 g granulated sugar

Prepare a boiling water bath and 4 half-pint/250 ml jars according to the process on page 10. Place the lids in a small saucepan, cover them with water, and simmer over very low heat.

Combine the chopped rhubarb with 3 cups/720 ml water in a medium pot and bring to a boil. Reduce the heat and simmer until the rhubarb is soft enough to be easily mashed with a wooden spoon, about 15 minutes.

Place a large fine-mesh sieve over a large bowl and strain the rhubarb and its juice through the sieve. Let the rhubarb drip undisturbed. Do your best to resist the urge to press the rhubarb pulp to help it release its liquid as this will result in cloudy syrup.

Discard the solids in the sieve and return the strained juice to the pot. Add the sugar and bring to a boil, skimming any foam that appears on the top.

Remove the pot from the heat and pour the hot syrup into the prepared jars, leaving $\frac{1}{2}$ inch/12 mm of headspace. Wipe the rims, apply the lids and rings, and process in a boiling water bath for 10 minutes (see page 11).

BLUEBERRY-LEMON SYRUP

DURING THE SUMMER, I OFTEN MAKE BLUEBERRY-studded pancakes. I make them only for myself since my husband had a bad encounter with blueberries as a child and won't touch them now. To turn this syrup into the perfect pancake topping, add a little cornstarch slurry and heat just until it thickens. For some reason, despite his aversion to the whole berry, Scott is happy to top his pancakes with this fruity syrup.

MAKES 4 (HALF-PINT/250 ML) JARS

3 pints/890 g blueberries
Zest and juice of 1 lemon
1³⁄₄ cup/350 g granulated sugar

Prepare a boiling water bath and 4 half-pint/250 ml jars according to the process on page 10. Place the lids in a small saucepan, cover them with water, and simmer over very low heat.

Place the blueberries in a medium pot and crush them with a potato masher. Add 3 cups/720 ml water and the lemon zest. Bring to a boil, then reduce the heat and simmer until the blueberries are soft and the liquid is a vivid purple, about 15 minutes.

Place a large fine-mesh sieve over a large bowl and strain the berries and their juice through the sieve. Let the berries drip undisturbed. Do your best to resist the urge to press the blueberry bits as this will result in a cloudy syrup.

Discard the solids in the sieve and return the strained juice to the pot. Add the lemon juice and sugar and bring to a boil, skimming any foam that appears on the top.

Remove the pot from the heat and pour the hot syrup into the prepared jars, leaving ¹⁄₂ inch/12 mm of headspace. Wipe the rims, apply the lids and rings, and process in a boiling water bath for 10 minutes (see page 11).

CRANBERRY SYRUP

THIS SYRUP IS A GREAT WAY TO USE UP POST-HOLIDAY cranberries (I can't be the only one who overbuys in anticipation of Thanksgiving and Christmas). The resulting syrup is quite thin, but has a sparkling, intense taste. I find that the thinner syrup works best for mixing into sparkling water and cocktails. However, if you want a thicker syrup, you can cook it down further until it turns sticky and similar in consistency to molasses.

MAKES 4 (HALF-PINT/250 ML) JARS

1 pound/455 g cranberries
2 cups/400 g granulated sugar

Prepare a boiling water bath and 4 half-pint/250 ml jars according to the process on page 10. Place the lids in a small saucepan, cover them with water, and simmer over very low heat.

Combine the cranberries with 3 cups/720 ml water in a medium pot and bring to a boil. Reduce the heat and simmer until the berries burst, about 10 minutes.

Place a large fine-mesh sieve over a large bowl and strain the cranberries and their juice through the sieve. Let the cranberries drip undisturbed. Do your best to resist the urge to press the berry mash to help it release its liquid as this will result in a cloudy syrup.

Discard the solids in the sieve and return the strained juice to the pot. Add the sugar and bring to a boil, skimming any foam that appears on the top.

Remove the pan from the heat and pour the hot syrup into the prepared jars, leaving ½ inch/12 mm of headspace. Wipe the rims, apply the lids and rings, and process in a boiling water bath for 10 minutes (see page 11).

WHOLE FRUIT

Y GRANDMA BUNNY WAS A SEASONAL EATER
long before it was cool. In her day, that's what everyone did.
During the early years of her marriage, she lived on a farm in Virginia, not too far outside of Washington, D.C. It was there that she took up canning and adopted the habit of dishing out her home-canned fruit for dessert.

Truly, I think she was on to something. Canned fruit feels a bit more special that just grabbing a pear or an apple from the kitchen fruit bowl. Thanks to the heat it experiences during processing, the fruit takes on a mellow, silky texture. If you've taken the time to tuck a bit of vanilla bean, a hunk of cinnamon stick, or a whole star anise into the jar, it will be bright with flavor. And of course, the bit of sugar or honey in the syrup adds sweetness. If you ask me, canned fruit is nearly perfect for dessert.

This section contains just a sampling of options for canning fruit. Once you work your way through these recipes, you'll find that there's a whole fruity world out there waiting to be explored. I have kept the syrups fairly light because I like to maintain the idea that I'm eating something healthy. However, if you want to make a more indulgent batch, you can amp up the amount of sweetener in your syrup.

CANNED ORANGE AND
GRAPEFRUIT SEGMENTS

I MADE A VERSION OF THESE WITH MANDARIN ORANGES in the first year of my blog. I was so proud of them until I opened the third jar, about a month after canning. The fruit had turned bitter and I ended up throwing out all remaining jars. I later learned that if you don't remove the white membrane that divides each section of the fruit, sooner or later it will turn everything in the jar inedibly bitter. I didn't want to give up canning citrus entirely, so I switched to a blend of oranges and grapefruit because their larger size makes it easier to remove those pesky membranes. As a happy bonus, they also happen to taste terrific together.

MAKES 4 (1-PINT/500 ML) JARS

3 pounds/1.4 kg navel oranges
3 pounds/1.4 kg ruby red grapefruit
1 cup/200 g granulated sugar

Prepare a boiling water bath and 4 regular-mouth 1-pint/500 ml jars according to the process on page 10. Place the lids in a small saucepan, cover them with water, and simmer over very low heat.

Segment the oranges and grapefruit according to the directions on page 000. Discard the peel and membrane.

Make the syrup by combining the sugar with 3 cups/720 ml water in a saucepan. Place over medium heat and stir until the sugar is dissolved. Bring to a gentle simmer and add the segmented citrus fruit. Heat the fruit until warmed through, about 4 to 5 minutes. Ladle the fruit and syrup into the prepared jars, leaving $\frac{1}{2}$ inch/12 mm headspace. Gently tap the jars on a towel-lined countertop to help loosen any bubbles before using a wooden chopstick to dislodge any remaining bubbles and add additional syrup, if necessary.

Wipe the rims, apply the lids and rings, and process in a boiling water bath for 10 minutes (see page 11).

BOOZY CANNED PEACHES ~⚬

CANNED PEACHES GENERALLY GET A BAD RAP. THE ones you buy at the grocery store typically manage to be both flavorless and slightly metallic. And often, home-canned peaches can look a little like a creature that has spent its life underwater. The thing is, however homely, a ripe peach canned in a slightly sweet syrup is just wonderful, particularly in March or April, when stone fruit is still months away. Add a slug of bourbon to each jar and prepare to be transported.

MAKES 4 (1-PINT/500 ML) JARS

6 pounds/2.7 kg peaches (preferably freestone)
1 lemon
1½ cups/300 g granulated sugar
1 cup bourbon, divided

Prepare a boiling water bath and 4 regular-mouth 1-pint/500 ml jars according to the process on page 10. Place the lids in a small saucepan, cover them with water, and simmer over very low heat.

Bring a large pot of water to a boil. While it heats, cut the peaches in half and remove the pits. Fill a large bowl two-thirds full with ice-cold water. Cut the lemon in half and squeeze the juice into the water. This is where your peaches will go when they come out of the hot water bath. The cold water stops the cooking and the lemon helps prevent the fruit from browning.

Working in batches, add the peach halves to the boiling water and cook for 60 seconds. Immediately transfer the peaches to the bowl filled with ice-cold water. Before adding the next batch of peaches to the pot, make sure to give the water a chance to come back up to boiling between batches. If the water isn't hot enough, you will have a hard time removing the skin during peeling.

Once all the peaches have been blanched and they are cool enough to handle, remove the skins with your fingers and return the fruit to the lemon water.

Combine the sugar with 3 cups/720 ml water in a large saucepan. Place over medium heat and stir until the sugar is dissolved. Bring to a gentle simmer.

While the syrup heats, pack the peeled peach halves, cut-side down into the *(continued)* prepared jars so that they overlap a bit. Use a wooden chopstick or narrow-head silicone spatula to help you layer them into the jars. It's best to use regular-mouth jars instead of wide-mouth jars in this instance, as the shoulders of the jars will help keep the peaches from floating out of the syrup after processing. Pack the peaches in as tightly as you can manage without damaging them.

When all the peaches are in the jars, ladle the hot syrup over them, leaving $1\frac{1}{2}$ inches/4 cm headspace so that there's room for the bourbon. Add $\frac{1}{4}$ cup/60 ml bourbon to each jar. Use a wooden chopstick to remove any air bubbles and, if necessary, add additional syrup to the jars so that each has $\frac{1}{2}$ inch/12 mm of headspace.

Wipe the rims, apply the lids and rings, and process in a boiling water bath for 25 minutes (see page 11).

GINGERY CANNED SECKEL PEARS

SECKEL PEARS ARE THOSE ADORABLE MINIATURE pears that you often see at farmers' markets and specialty grocers. They have firm flesh and a mellow, crisp taste that works well with this gingery syrup. I find pear skin inoffensive, so I don't peel pears prior to canning. If you're not a fan, feel free to peel before packing them into the jars. For a quick dessert for a party or potluck, make a simple cake batter, pour it into a greased 8x8-inch pan, and push these pear halves into the surface in a grid pattern. It makes for a tender, wonderfully flavored cake.

MAKES 4 (1-PINT/500 ML) JARS

5 pounds/2.3 kg Seckel pears
$1\frac{1}{2}$ cups/300 g granulated sugar
1 cup/240 ml ginger juice (see page 31)

Prepare a boiling water bath and 4 regular-mouth 1-pint/500 ml jars according to the process on page 10. Place the lids in a small saucepan, cover them with water, and simmer over very low heat.

Cut the pears in half and remove the seeds and blossom end of the fruit using a melon baller. Make the syrup by combining the sugar with the ginger juice and 2 cups/480 ml water in a medium saucepan. Place over medium heat and stir until the sugar is dissolved.

While the syrup heats, pack the pear halves, cut-side down, into the prepared jars. Use a wooden chopstick or narrow-head silicone spatula to help you layer them into the jars. It's best to use regular-mouth jars instead of wide-mouth jars in this instance, as the shoulders of the jars will help keep the pears from floating out of the syrup after processing. Pack the pears in as tightly as you can manage without damaging them.

When all the pears are in the jars, ladle the hot syrup over them, leaving $1/2$ inch/12 mm headspace. Gently tap the jars on a towel-lined countertop to help loosen any bubbles before using a wooden chopstick to dislodge any remaining bubbles and add additional syrup, if necessary.

Wipe the rims, apply the lids and rings, and process in a boiling water bath for 25 minutes (see page 11).

Note: Because they're so small, Seckel pears can also be canned whole. This is a great technique when you're overwhelmed by fruit and short on time. Wash the pears well, remove the stems, pack them into quart (1 liter) jars, cover with syrup, and process for 30 minutes. If you opt for this technique, you'll need to increase the amount of syrup by half.

PLUMS IN HONEY SYRUP

THESE WHOLE CANNED PLUMS HAVE SAVED ME
from uninspired breakfasts, lunches, and dinners more than once.
On the weekends, I will turn them into compote for pancakes or waf-
fles. On weekdays, these sweet plums are wonderful stirred into morning
oatmeal or with a dish of cottage cheese for lunch. Around dinnertime,
combine them with some sautéed onions and a splash of vinegar for a sweet
and tart pan sauce for meat or grilled vegetables. Finally, the syrup makes
a fabulous addition to glasses of sparkling water or cocktails. The canning
process does the work of cooking the plums, so the pits are easy to pinch
out.

MAKES 4 (1-PINT/500 ML) JARS

1 cup/240 ml honey
3 pounds/1.4 kg small, sweet plums
4 cinnamon sticks (optional)
1 whole vanilla bean, cut into 4 pieces (optional)

Prepare a boiling water bath and 4 regular-mouth 1-pint/500 ml jars according to the
process on page 10. Place the lids in a small saucepan, cover them with water, and
simmer over very low heat.

In a medium saucepan, combine the honey with 3 cups/720 ml water and bring to
a simmer.

Wash and dry the plums thoroughly and pack them tightly into the prepared jars. If
you've chosen to add the cinnamon or vanilla, tuck a length of either (or both) in the
jars at this time.

When all the plums are in the jars, ladle the hot syrup over them, leaving ½ inch/12
mm of headspace. Gently tap the jars on a towel-lined countertop to help loosen any
bubbles before using a wooden chopstick to dislodge any remaining bubbles and
add additional syrup, if necessary.

Wipe the rims, apply the lids and rings, and process in a boiling water bath for 20
minutes (see page 11).

Plums in Honey Syrup
and Boozy Canned Peaches

SPICED APPLESAUCE

TO ME, APPLESAUCE IS THE QUINTESSENTIAL FALL food. I have fond memories of wandering the antique apple orchard at the Bybee-Howell House on Sauvie Island, bundled up in layers against the chill, gathering windfall apples. Now my apples come from the orchards around Philadelphia but the ritual of chopping and simmering into sauce is the same. I like having supplies of this around for baking, cooking, and late-night snacking.

MAKES 4 (1-PINT/500 ML) JARS

5 pounds/2.3 kg apples (a mix of varieties is
  best so choose your favorites; see note on page 47)
$\frac{1}{2}$ cup/120 ml apple juice or cider
2 whole star anise
1 tablespoon ground cinnamon
1 teaspoon freshly grated nutmeg
$\frac{1}{2}$ teaspoon ground cloves
1 cup/200 g (about) granulated sugar

Prepare a boiling water bath and 4 regular-mouth 1-pint/500 ml jars according to the process on page 10. Place the lids in a small saucepan, cover them with water, and simmer over very low heat.

Peel and chop the apples. Put them in a large, nonreactive pot. Add the apple cider and star anise. Cover and bring to a simmer over medium heat, stirring regularly, until the fruit has broken down, about 15 to 20 minutes.

Remove the star anise. Using a potato masher or immersion blender, break down the fruit until it is a chunky sauce. Add the cinnamon, nutmeg, and cloves. Taste and add as much sugar as your taste buds determine necessary.

Pour the applesauce into the prepared jars, leaving $\frac{3}{4}$ inch/18 mm headspace. Wipe the rims, apply the lids and rings, and process in a boiling water bath for 15 minutes (see page 11).

When the processing time is up, remove the canning pot from the heat and remove the lid. Let the jars sit in the pot for an additional 5 minutes to prevent the applesauce from reacting to the temperature change and bubbling out of the jars.

BING CHERRIES IN RED WINE SYRUP

IF YOU'RE THE TYPE WHO SEARCHES OUT THE WINE-soaked fruit in the bottom of a pitcher of sangria, these cherries are for you. Don't use a super expensive bottle of wine; anything that's drinkable and not too sweet works well. Try these over ice cream or with a slice of pound cake.

MAKES 4 (1-PINT/500 ML) JARS

2 cups/480 ml dry red wine
1 ½ cups/300 g granulated sugar
1 vanilla bean, split and scraped
Zest of 1 lemon
4 pounds/1.8 kg Bing cherries, pitted

Prepare a boiling water bath and 4 regular-mouth 1-pint/500 ml jars according to the process on page 10. Place the lids in a small saucepan, cover them with water, and simmer over very low heat.

In a medium saucepan, combine the red wine, 1 cup/240 ml water, the sugar, vanilla bean and seeds, and lemon zest. Bring to a simmer over medium heat, stirring until the sugar is dissolved.

Pack the pitted cherries into the prepared jars and ladle in the hot syrup, leaving ½ inch/12 mm headspace. Gently tap the jars on a towel-lined countertop to help loosen any bubbles before using a wooden chopstick to dislodge any remaining bubbles and add additional syrup, if necessary.

Wipe the rims, apply the lids and rings, and process in a boiling water bath for 25 minutes (see page 11).

HONEYED APRICOTS

PEACHES ARE NICE, NECTARINES ARE LOVELY, BUT as far as I'm concerned, apricots are the stars of the summer stone fruit season. Sweet, tart, fragrant, and just slightly floral, good apricots are transformational. During their season, I like to make apricot jam and butter, but I never fail to put some up in a honey syrup. Try these apricots halves stirred into yogurt, alongside cottage cheese, or in a fruity crisp at holiday time.

MAKES 4 (1-PINT/500 ML) JARS

1 ¼ cups/300 ml honey
4 pounds/1.8 kg ripe apricots

Prepare a boiling water bath and 4 regular-mouth 1-pint/500 ml jars according to the process on page 10. Place the lids in a small saucepan, cover them with water, and simmer over very low heat.

In a medium saucepan, combine the honey with 3 cups/720 ml water and bring to a simmer.

Wash and dry the apricots thoroughly, cut them in half, and remove the pits. Tightly pack the apricot halves, cut-side down, into the prepared jars.

When all the apricots are in the jars, ladle the hot syrup over them, leaving ½ inch/12 mm of headspace.

Gently tap the jars on a towel-lined countertop to help loosen any bubbles before using a wooden chopstick to dislodge any remaining bubbles and add additional syrup, if necessary.

Wipe the rims, apply the lids and rings, and process in a boiling water bath for 20 minutes (see page 11).

BLUEBERRIES IN SYRUP

BLUEBERRIES GROW REALLY WELL IN MY NEIGH-
boring state of New Jersey. Because they're so cheap and good, I go
a little crazy each summer and buy far more than I can possibly eat
before they go bad. I make Blueberry Jam (page 41), Blueberry Butter
(page 56), and put some up whole in syrup. Canning them whole in syrup
gives you a world of options beyond toast, pancakes, and yogurt. I like to
stir them into muffin batter or bake them in a freeform pie for Thanksgiving or Christmas.

MAKES 4 (1-PINT/500 ML) JARS

1 cup/200 g granulated sugar
4 pounds/1.8 kg blueberries

Prepare a boiling water bath and 4 regular-mouth 1-pint/500 ml jars according to the
process on page 10. Place the lids in a small saucepan, cover them with water, and
simmer over very low heat.

In a large saucepan, combine the sugar with 3 cups/720 ml water and bring to a
simmer.

Bring a large pot of water to a boil and blanch the blueberries for 30 seconds. Drain
them well and pour the berries into the saucepan with the syrup. Stir to combine.

Ladle the fruit and syrup into the prepared jars, leaving $\frac{1}{2}$ inch/12 mm of headspace. Make sure that the fruit is submerged in the syrup. Gently tap the jars on a
towel-lined countertop to help loosen any bubbles before using a wooden chopstick
to dislodge any remaining bubbles and add additional syrup, if necessary.

Wipe the rims, apply the lids and rings, and process in a boiling water bath for 15
minutes (see page 11).

GRANOLA IN JARS

WHEN I WAS IN THE FIFTH GRADE, I DECIDED THAT
I was done with sandwiches. My mother did not take the news
well, as she depended on a rotating schedule of turkey with cheddar and peanut butter and honey to keep me fed during the school day. After
much negotiation and a few tears (entirely on my part), we settled on a new
lunchtime staple: a cup of yogurt, topped with a nutty granola.

While the yogurt rarely changed (Tillamook Creamery's vanilla bean), I was
willing to mix it up when it came to the granola. If my mom had time to make
it, I'd have Melinda's GORP (see page 198). Other days, I'd opt for the maple
granola that came from the bulk bins at Food Front in northwest Portland.

To this day, my capacity for eating granola is fairly unlimited. I always have
at least one batch on my kitchen counter, stashed in a half-gallon Ball jar. I
appreciate how versatile it is (eat it with yogurt, milk, applesauce, or straight
from your palm) and how easy it is to make from scratch (and oh so much
cheaper than buying it!).

As you tackle your own granola projects, keep in mind that these recipes are
really just starting places. Feel free to make adjustments, so that you end up
with a finished product that you love.

Note: There are a couple of ways to get those crunchy granola clusters we
all crave. One method is to mix in a couple of lightly beaten egg whites to
your batch prior to baking. Another option: After baking, scrape all the granola to the center of your baking sheet and press it down with your spatula.
Whichever method you use, let the granola sit undisturbed until completely
cool and clustery.

GINGER WALNUT GRANOLA

WHOLE FOODS USED TO CARRY A GINGER GRANOLA in their bulk section that my husband loved. Then one day, it just wasn't there anymore. So I set out to recreate a version as close to it as I could get. He quickly changed allegiances to this recipe and now we nearly always have a jar on the counter for morning meals and snacks.

MAKES 6 CUPS/600 G

4 cups/340 g old-fashioned rolled oats

1 1/2 cups/170 g chopped raw walnuts

1 teaspoon ground ginger

1/4 teaspoon sea salt

1/4 cup/60 ml sunflower oil (or other neutral oil)

1/2 cup/120 ml cane syrup (such as Lyle's Golden Syrup or Steen's) or agave nectar

2 egg whites, beaten until frothy

1 cup/140 g finely chopped crystallized ginger

Preheat oven to 325°F/165°C/gas 3.

In a large mixing bowl, combine the oats, walnuts, ground ginger, and salt. Use your hands to toss together. Pour the sunflower oil into a glass measuring cup and swirl it around before adding it to the oat mixture. Using the same, unwashed cup measure the cane syrup. The residual oil will help the syrup exit the cup.

Use a silicone spatula to work the oil and cane syrup into the oats and nuts. When it is well integrated, add the beaten egg whites and toss to coat. The egg white helps the granola form clusters, a key element to an appealing, crunchy granola.

Spread the granola out on a rimmed baking sheet and place in the oven. Bake the granola until it is golden brown, about 30 to 35 minutes, stirring the granola every 10 minutes so that it bakes evenly.

Remove the granola from the oven. Sprinkle the crystallized ginger over the hot granola and quickly stir it in. Leave the granola to cool for several hours, or even overnight, so that the crunchy clusters have plenty of time to set up.

When the granola is completely cool, break it up into small clusters and store it in an airtight container. It will keep for a week to 10 days.

MELINDA'S GORP GRANOLA
(GOOD OLD RAISINS AND PEANUTS)

BACK IN THE EARLY 1970S, MY MOM'S FRIEND MEL-
inda had a small business making GORP, a most beloved hippie
food. One day, on her way home with a month's worth of ingredients in her VW Beetle, Melinda was rear-ended. The force of the impact
sent oats, nuts, raisins, oil, and honey flying all over the interior of the
car. Even after the repairs were completed, the car was never the same.
She stopped making her GORP soon after that, but shared the recipe with
my mother before hanging up her spatula for good.

MAKES 6 CUPS/600 G

2 cups/170 g old-fashioned rolled oats
1 cup/150 g raw, unsalted peanuts
1/4 cup/35 g sesame seeds
1/2 cup/55 g raw sunflower seeds
1/2 cup/40 g unsweetened dried flaked coconut
1/4 cup/30 g wheat germ
1/4 cup/60 ml sunflower oil (or other neutral oil)
1/2 cup/120 ml honey
1 cup raisins/170 g

Preheat oven to 325°F/165°C/gas 3.

In a large bowl, combine the oats, peanuts, sesame seeds, sunflower seeds, flaked
coconut, and wheat germ. Pour the sunflower oil into a glass measuring cup and swirl
it around before adding it to the bowl. Using the same, unwashed cup, measure the
honey and add it to the bowl. The residual oil will help the honey exit the cup. Using a
silicone spatula stir everything together until evenly coated and then spread the mixture out on a rimmed baking sheet.

Bake the granola for 30 minutes, turning it with a spatula every 10 minutes so that
it browns evenly. It is done when nuts are deeply toasted. Remove the baking sheet
from the oven and return the granola to the mixing bowl. Add the raisins and stir to
combine. Stir gently several times as it cools, so that it doesn't clump.

When the granola is completely cool, store it in an airtight container.

MAPLE PECAN GRANOLA
WITH BLUEBERRIES

THIS GRANOLA IS MY ANSWER TO A SECRET DESIRE to eat oatmeal cookies for breakfast. Because there are so few ingredients, the flavor of the butter really shines through so make sure yours is fresh. In addition to all the usual uses for this granola, I like to sprinkle it on top of warm applesauce to mimic the flavor of a freshly baked fruit crisp.

MAKES 5 CUPS/500 G

¼ cup/55 g unsalted butter, melted and cooled

3 cups/255 g old-fashioned rolled oats

1 cup/115 g chopped pecans

¼ teaspoon sea salt

½ teaspoon freshly grated nutmeg

½ cup/120 ml real maple syrup

½ cup/75 g dried unsweetened blueberries

Preheat oven to 325°F/165°C/gas 3.

Heat the butter just until it melts and set aside.

In large bowl, combine the oats, pecans, salt, and nutmeg. Add the melted butter and maple syrup and stir to combine. Spread the granola mixture out on a rimmed baking sheet and bake until the nuts in the granola are a deep brown, about 25 to 30 minutes, stirring 2 to 3 times during baking to ensure even browning.

Remove the baking sheet from the oven and let the granola cool. When the granola is just barely warm, sprinkle the dried blueberries over the top and stir them in.

When the granola is completely cool, store it in an airtight container.

Note: Because this recipe includes butter, it will have a shorter shelf life than some other granolas. Eat or refrigerate within 4 to 5 days.

CRANBERRY ORANGE GRANOLA

THE INSPIRATION FOR THIS GRANOLA CAME FROM a scone recipe my mother often uses. Just barely sweet and fragrant with the scent of orange zest, they are studded with toasted walnuts and dried cranberries. Delicious when first baked, they rapidly lose their appeal as they age, rendering them impossible to eat the second day. This recipe offers similar flavors in a hardier format.

MAKES 6 CUPS/600 G

3 cups/255 g old-fashioned rolled oats
1 cup/110 g sliced almonds
1 cup/115 g chopped raw walnuts
$^1/_3$ cup/50 g poppy seeds
Zest of 1 orange
$^1/_4$ cup/60 ml sunflower oil (or other neutral oil)
$^1/_2$ cup/120 ml honey
$^1/_4$ cup/60 ml orange juice
1 cup/120 g dried cranberries

Preheat oven to 325°F/165°C/gas 3.

In a large bowl, combine the oats, almonds, walnuts, poppy seeds, and orange zest. Use your hands to toss everything together.

Pour the sunflower oil into a glass measuring cup and swirl it around before adding it to the bowl. Using the same, unwashed cup, measure the honey and add it to the bowl. The residual oil will help the honey exit the cup. Add the orange juice and stir everything together until evenly coated. Spread the mixture out on a rimmed baking sheet.

Bake until the granola is crisp and brown, about 30 to 35 minutes, stirring 2 to 3 times during baking to ensure even browning.

Remove the pan from the oven. Scatter the dried cranberries over the cereal and gently stir to incorporate.

When the granola is completely cool, store it in an airtight container. It will keep for a week to 10 days.

CRUNCHY BUCKWHEAT GRANOLA

WHEN SHE WAS A YOUNG WIDOW WITH THREE children, my great-grandmother opened a Russian teahouse in Philadelphia's theater district. A family endeavor for nearly fifty years, it was long since closed by the time I was born. I grew up with the old menus, rich with blintzes, borscht, and buttered kasha with bowties. Thanks to this family history, I've long looked for ways to eat more kasha. This granola gives me a delicious way to do just that and I'm certain my great-grandmother would approve.

MAKES 5 CUPS/500 G

2 cups/170 g old-fashioned rolled oats

1/2 cup/55 g sliced almonds

3/4 cup/120 g toasted buckwheat groats (kasha)

3/4 cup/85 g raw sunflower seeds

1/2 cup/60 g unsweetened dried flaked coconut

1/4 teaspoon sea salt

1 teaspoon ground cinnamon

1/2 teaspoon freshly grated nutmeg

1/4 cup/60 ml sunflower oil (or other neutral oil)

1/2 cup/120 ml honey

1/2 cup/85 g raisins

Preheat oven to 325°F/165°C/gas 3.

In a large bowl, combine the oats, almonds, buckwheat, sunflower seeds, flaked coconut, salt, cinnamon, and nutmeg. Toss it all together to combine.

Measure the sunflower oil in a large cup and swirl it around before adding it to the bowl. Using the same, unwashed cup, measure the honey and add it to the bowl. Stir everything together until evenly coated. Spread the mixture out on a rimmed baking sheet.

Bake until the granola is crisp and toasted, about 30 to 35 minutes, stirring 2 to 3 times during baking to ensure even browning.

Remove the granola from the oven. Gently stir in the raisins. If you want the granola to form clusters, mound the still-warm granola into the center of the baking sheet to cool. When the granola is completely cool store it in an airtight container. It will keep for a week to 10 days.

NUT BUTTERS

FROM MY EARLIEST DAYS AS AN EATER, I'VE BEEN a peanut butter lover. From kindergarten through third grade, I ate half a peanut butter-and-honey sandwich on whole wheat for lunch. My mother believed in the nutritional aspects of peanut butter and always spread a thick, protein-packed layer on every sandwich.

Despite the fact that peanut butter has always been a regular player in my diet, it took me until my thirties to realize that there was a world of nut butters beyond my beloved peanut. What's more, nearly all of them could be made at home in my sturdy, hand-me-down food processor.

In making batch after batch of nut butters, I've learned that the tastiest nut butters come from freshly roasted nuts, so all these recipes start with raw nuts and include a roasting step. It's best to make nut butters in fairly small batches, as the flavors are at their best within the first week. The yields on these recipes top out at 1^1/2 cups/ (380 g) of butter. If you have a larger capacity food processor, you can double the recipes, but I strongly encourage you to make only as much butter as you and your family can eat in a week or two.

As you process the nuts, they will pass through several stages. First, they'll resemble chopped nuts. Then they'll transition to a cornmeal-like state. Last, just before they achieve butter consistency, the contents of the food processor will resemble a really dry paste. You might begin to despair that you'll never achieve a proper butter consistency. Fear not. Keep processing.

At times, the nascent butter will form a ball in the bowl of the food processor. Just stop the motor, use a wooden spatula (food processors are really hard on plastic and silicone implements) to break up the clusters and continue with the processing. If you're really struggling to achieve the right consistency, just add another drizzle of oil and keep on chugging.

Soon enough, you too will find yourself breezing past the expensive jars of exotic spreadable nut products in the grocery store, smug in the knowledge that the ones you make yourself are so much better a butter.

CINNAMON VANILLA
SUNFLOWER BUTTER

IN THE WEEKS BEFORE I GOT MARRIED, I HANDLED the wedding stress by buying and eating vast quantities of nut butters. It didn't do good things for the fit of my dress, but it made that very DIY day far more manageable from a stress perspective. It was during that period that I discovered a particularly magnificent line of sunflower butters made in Michigan. They're not sold in my area, so with shipping, each jar cost nearly $20. The version below does a bang-up job of satisfying my craving, while ringing up somewhere south of $5 for nearly the same volume of butter.

MAKES 1½ CUPS/380 G

2 cups/225 g raw sunflower seeds
¼ cup/60 ml sunflower oil, divided
½ teaspoon sea salt, plus more as needed
2 tablespoons vanilla bean paste, plus more as needed
3 teaspoons ground cinnamon, plus more as needed

Preheat oven to 325°F/165°C/gas 3.

Spread the sunflower seeds out on a rimmed baking sheet. Roast in the oven until the sunflower seeds are fragrant and golden brown, about 25 to 30 minutes, stirring the seeds at least twice during baking to ensure even roasting.

Remove the baking sheet from the oven and let the sunflower seeds cool 10 minutes. When they're cool enough to handle, pour the toasted sunflower seeds into the bowl of a food processor. Add 1 tablespoon sunflower oil and 1/2 teaspoon sea salt and begin to run the processor.

As the motor runs and the sunflower seeds break down, drizzle in the remaining 3 tablespoons of sunflower oil.

Continue to process in 10- to 20-second intervals, stopping the motor and removing the lid after each to break up any clumps and scrape down the sides of the processor.

As the contents of the processor begin to look like butter, add the vanilla paste and

(continued)

cinnamon to the bowl of the processor and pulse to incorporate. Taste after they're fully incorporated and add an additional pinch of cinnamon, vanilla, or salt if necessary.

Scrape the sunflower seed butter into a jar and store in the refrigerator. It will keep up to 1 month.

HONEY-ROASTED PEANUT BUTTER

THIS BUTTER COMBINES BOTH ASPECTS OF MY FAV-favorite childhood sandwich in a single spread. In addition to being terrific in all the applications you're used to, I like to take it to potlucks, paired with a platter of crisp apple and pear slices (toss the fruit in a little lemon juice to prevent browning). It's amazing how impressed people are by this slightly sweet, homemade peanut butter.

MAKES 1½ CUPS/380 G

2 cups/290 g raw peanuts
3 tablespoons honey, divided
3 tablespoons peanut oil, divided
1½ teaspoons sea salt, divided

Preheat oven to 325°F/165°C/gas 3. Line a baking sheet with a silicone baking mat or parchment paper.

Spread the peanuts on the prepared baking sheet. Drizzle with 2 tablespoons honey, toss evenly to coat and roast in the oven until the nuts are golden brown, about 25 to 30 minutes, stirring the peanuts at least twice during baking to ensure even roasting.

Remove the baking sheet from the oven and let the peanuts cool for at least 10 minutes. When they're cool enough to handle, pour the honey-roasted peanuts into the bowl of a food processor. Add 1 tablespoon peanut oil and 1 teaspoon sea salt and begin to run the processor.

As the motor runs and the peanuts break down, drizzle in the remaining 2 tablespoons peanut oil.

Continue to process in 20- to 30-second intervals, stopping the motor and removing the lid after each interval to break up any clumps and scrape down the sides of the processor.

When the contents of the bowl resemble peanut butter, stop the motor, remove the lid, and taste. Add the remaining tablespoon honey and ½ teaspoon salt only if you deem it necessary (the beauty of making your own nut butter is that you can make it just how you like it).

Scrape the peanut butter into a jar and store in the refrigerator. It will keep up to 1 month.

MAPLE ALMOND BUTTER

HAVE A DEAR FRIEND WHO ADORES ALMOND BUTTER. For the first decade of our friendship, I didn't quite understand why she raved about it so much. I found it to be sort of stodgy, bitter and unyielding, not nearly as good as my beloved peanut butter. Then I tried making it myself. The butter that came out of my food processor was smooth, rich and entirely delicious. Suddenly, I completely understood her appreciation and was slathering it on toast, bananas, and even the occasional tortilla chip.

MAKES 1½ CUPS/380 G

2 cups/290 g raw almonds
2 tablespoons real maple syrup
¼ teaspoon sea salt
2 tablespoons walnut oil (or any other complementary neutral oil), divided

Preheat oven to 325°F/165°C/gas 3. Line a rimmed baking sheet with a silicone baking mat or parchment paper.

Spread the almonds on the prepared baking sheet. Drizzle the maple syrup over the almonds and toss the nuts with your fingers so that they get evenly coated. Roast in the oven until the nuts go brown and the maple syrup darkens, about 20 minutes, tossing at least once during baking to ensure even roasting.

(continued)

Remove the baking sheet from the oven and let the maple-roasted almonds cool for 10 to 15 minutes.

When they're cool enough to handle, pour the maple-roasted nuts into the bowl of a food processor and pulse to begin breaking them up. Add the salt and a drizzle of the walnut oil and run the processor 30 to 45 seconds. Remove the lid and scrape down the sides. Repeat this process-drizzle-scrape procedure until the almonds have broken down into butter. You may not need all the oil; it will depend on the moisture content of the almonds.

Scrape the almond butter into a jar and store in the refrigerator. It will keep up to 1 month.

CHOCOLATE HAZELNUT BUTTER

EVERYONE HAS A STORY ABOUT THE FIRST TIME they tasted Nutella. I lost my chocolate and hazelnut-spread innocence when I was in college. As I got older, I didn't lose my taste for it, but I did lose my incredible tolerance for sweets. This version takes all the goodness of that iconic spread and transforms it into something slightly less sugary but no less delicious.

MAKES A GENEROUS 1½ CUPS/380 G

2 cups/270 g hazelnuts

2 teaspoons walnut oil (or any other complementary neutral oil)

3 ounces/85 g dark chocolate, melted

¼ cup/20 g cocoa powder

1 vanilla bean, split and scraped

⅔ cup/70 g confectioners' sugar

¼ teaspoon sea salt

Preheat oven to 350°F/180°C/gas 4.

Spread the hazelnuts out on the prepared baking sheet. Roast in the oven until the nuts are fragrant, about 10 to 12 minutes, shaking the pan to stir up the nuts at least once during baking to ensure even roasting.

Remove the baking sheet from the oven and pour the nuts into a large, fine-mesh strainer and gently shake it. This helps loosen the skins of the hazelnuts. Alternatively, let the nuts cool for 10 minutes on the baking sheet. When the nuts are cool enough to handle, you can bundle them in a clean kitchen towel and rub vigorously to aid the removal of the skins. They don't all have to be removed, but they can impart a bitter flavor if too many remain.

Pour the nuts into the bowl of a food processor and process until they resemble cornmeal. Add the walnut oil and melted chocolate, and pulse to combine.

Remove the lid, scrape down the sides, and add the remaining ingredients. Pulse to combine and then remove the lid and scrape down the sides of the bowl again. Repeat this process-scrape procedure until your product resembles butter.

Scrape the butter into a jar and store in the refrigerator. It will keep up to 1 month.

Rosemary Salt

OTHER FOODS in JARS

ARS AREN'T JUST FOR PRESERVES. THEY DO GOOD work as receptacles for leftovers, can serve as a to-go mug in a pinch and also make excellent canisters for dry goods, (if you have issues with pantry moths, keeping all your dry goods in jars will greatly reduce their spread). I often take jars with me to grocery stores with bulk sections so that I can avoid using a plastic bag and dispense my oatmeal directly into the jar where it belongs (before filling, make sure to take your jar to the customer service department so that they can weigh it and give you a tare for the jar. That way, you won't have to pay for the weight of the jars in addition to the contents).

One tool that works just as well for general jar filling as it does for canning activities is a wide mouth funnel. It makes getting mixes, grains, and beans into the jars far less messy and frustrating. The best way to pack dry goods into a jar is to fill it halfway, apply the lid, and then gently tap the bottom of the jar with the heel of your hand. This helps settle the contents of the jar to make a bit more space, and it also helps to prevent a mess.

Because I make so much jam, I often give it away to friends and family. On special occasions, I like to pair the jam with a complementary mix to round out the present. Of course, many of those mixes are packaged in jars. Here are a few of my favorites.

MO'S FAMOUS WHOLE GRAIN PANCAKE MIX ～♈

ASK ANYONE OF HIS ACQUAINTANCE AND THEY'LL tell you that my father is a pancake expert. During his early twenties, he worked as a short order cook at IHOP, and after eating yet another doughy pancake, he determined that he could do better. So, for a period spanning multiple years, he devoted himself to the creation of a better pancake mix. By the time I was born, he had worked out the bones of this recipe. It's so good that it became our family's holiday gift for friends, family, and neighbors. Packaged up and combined with a jar of jam or maple syrup, people are always delighted to receive their annual batch of Mo's Famous Pancakes. Don't let the long list of ingredients scare you off. They're nearly all available at the grocery store, including the wheat germ, which you can buy pre-toasted.

MAKES 2 (1-QUART/1 LITER) JARS DRY MIX

2 cups/255 g whole-wheat flour

3 cups/385 g whole-wheat pastry flour

2 cups/230 g toasted wheat germ

1 cup/140 g cornmeal

1 cup/200 g millet, toasted (see note)

$^3/_4$ cup/150 g granulated sugar

2 tablespoons salt

3 tablespoons baking powder

Combine all the ingredients in a large bowl and gently whisk to combine. Divide the mix between 2 clean 1-quart/1 liter jars and store in the refrigerator (cold storage will greatly extend the life of all those whole grains).

To make the pancakes, whisk 3 large eggs in a medium bowl, then mix in 1 cup/240 ml milk and 2 tablespoons light vegetable oil. Fold in 2 cups of the pancake mix. If it seems too thick, add a splash more milk. Lightly oil a griddle and set over medium heat. When the griddle is hot, spoon approximately $^1/_4$ cup batter per cake onto the

(continued)

griddle and watch for bubbles to form around the edges of the cakes, about 3 minutes. When some of the bubbles pop and stay open, flip the cakes and cook another 1 to 2 minutes. Serve with maple syrup (real only, please), jam, and yogurt or honey. This will yield about 12 pancakes.

If giving this mix as a gift, print these instructions on a tag and include it with the jar.
Note: To make toasted millet, spread on a rimmed baking sheet and bake for 8 to 10 minutes at 350°F. Watch carefully as it toasts, as it can go from barely cooked to burnt very quickly. Let it cool completely before adding it to the mix. It introduces a wonderful, nutty crunch.

TY'S HERBED BEER BREAD MIX

WHEN I GOT MARRIED, ONE OF THE BEST GIFTS we received came from Ty Myers, the mother of a dear friend. She came to the wedding with a reusable grocery bag filled with half a dozen quart jars. In each jar was a different homemade baking mix and every jar had a tag fastened to it, describing how to transform those dry goods into something delicious. Soon after the wedding, Ty shared several of her mix recipes with me and with her permission, I've included two here. The first is a quick bread that gets its lift from the reaction of baking powder and beer. It's wonderful hot out of the oven or toasted and buttered.

MAKES 1 (1-QUART/1 LITER) JAR (FOR 1 LOAF BREAD)

3 cups/385 g all-purpose flour

3 tablespoons granulated sugar

1½ tablespoons baking powder

1 tablespoon dried parsley flakes

1 tablespoon dried sage

1 tablespoon dried rosemary

1 tablespoon dried thyme

1½ teaspoons salt

Combine all the ingredients in a medium bowl and gently whisk to combine. Pour the mix into a clean 1-quart/1 liter jar. Apply the lid and store in a cool, dry place until ready to use or give.

To use this mix: Preheat oven to 350°F/180°C/gas 4. Butter a 9x5-inch loaf pan. In a medium bowl, combine Ty's Herbed Beer Bread Mix with 12 ounces/360 ml warm beer and stir until just combined (a few lumps are OK). Pour into the prepared pan and dot with 2 tablespoons butter, cut into small pieces. Bake for 45 to 50 minutes, until the crust is golden brown.

If giving this mix as a gift, print these instructions on a tag and include it with the jar.

SHAY'S CHOCOLATE CAKE IN A JAR

TY'S DAUGHTER SHAY MAKES THIS CAKE FOR EVERY birthday or special occasion. I've eaten it for several of my birthdays and cannot get enough, especially when it's topped with peanut butter frosting. I try to keep at least one jar of the mix on hand in my pantry as it's perfect for any cake emergency.

MAKES 1 (1-QUART/1 LITER) JAR (ONE 9X13-INCH CAKE)

1 $\frac{1}{2}$ cups/300 g granulated sugar
2 cups/255 g all-purpose flour
$\frac{3}{4}$ cup/70 g black cocoa powder (not Dutch process)
2 teaspoons baking soda
1 teaspoon baking powder
1 heaping tablespoon instant coffee

Starting with the sugar, layer the ingredients into a clean 1-quart/1 liter jar. Make sure to gently tap the bottom of the jar between each layer, to ensure that everything will fit. No matter what, it will be a snug fit. Apply the lid and store in a cool, dry place until ready to use or give.

To use this mix: Preheat the oven to 350°F/180°C/gas 4. Butter a 9x13-inch cake
(*continued*)

pan. In a large bowl, beat together 2 large eggs, ½ cup/120 ml unsweetened apple-sauce, 2 cups/480 ml hot water, and 1 teaspoon vanilla extract. Add Ty's Chocolate Cake in a Jar mix and stir until combined. Pour the batter into the prepared pan (batter will be runny). Bake for 35 to 40 minutes, until a toothpick or cake tester comes out clean. When the cake is cool, top with your frosting of choice. Peanut butter or raspberry flavors go particularly well with this cake.

If giving this mix as a gift, print these instructions on a tag and include it with the jar. Note: Make sure to search out true black cocoa powder for this cake. It gives it a rich, chocolaty flavor and color. If you can't find it at your local grocery store, King Arthur Flour (kingarthurflour.com) sells it.

TRIO OF FLAVORED SALTS

At any given time, I have several jars of infused salts in my kitchen. I like to use sea salt for these homemade flavored salts as it feels the most receptive to the absorption of the flavors. For the salt blends that are higher in moisture, dry them briefly in the oven to ensure that they don't form a solid block of salt once put into the jar. Here are a few of my favorites.

VANILLA SALT

IN RECENT DAYS, IT HAS BECOME THE TREND TO ADD A touch of sea salt to baked goods, caramels, and other sweets. Add yet another layer of flavor by infusing the fragrance of vanilla into the salt you sprinkle atop your desserts.

MAKES 2 (HALF-PINT/250 ML) JARS

3 vanilla beans, split and scraped
1 cup/175 g flaky sea salt (such as Maldon)

Combine the vanilla bean seeds with the sea salt in a bowl. Use your fingertips to rub the vanilla into the salt. Divide the vanilla bean pods between 2 half-pint/250 ml jars and pour the salt over them, dividing equally. Apply the lids and store in a cool, dark place.

LEMON SALT

DURING JANUARY AND FEBRUARY, I GO A LITTLE citrus crazy in an attempt to ward off the wintertime blues. This infused salt is a good way to capture the aromatic oils that exist in the skins of the lemons. Try this flavored salt on grilled fish or sprinkled over popcorn.

MAKES 2 (HALF-PINT/250 ML) JARS

Finely grated zest of 2 lemons
1 cup/190 g finely milled sea salt

Preheat the oven to 200°F/95°C (or lower if you have that option on your oven).

Combine the lemon zest and salt in a bowl. Use your fingertips to rub the lemon zest into the salt. Spread the salt mixture on a foil-lined rimmed baking sheet and bake until you can smell the fragrance of the lemons and the salt feels dry to the touch, about 20 minutes.

Remove the pan from the oven and let the salt cool at room temperature. When the salt is cool, break up any chunks that may have formed and pour it into 2 half-pint/250 ml jars. Store in a cool, dark place.

ROSEMARY SALT

NO MATTER WHERE THEY LIVE, MY PARENTS ALWAYS have rosemary growing in their yard. Its scent is linked in my mind with family and home-cooked food. For those of you who don't have regular access to fresh rosemary, this salt is a good way to keep its bright fragrance and flavor close by. I particularly like it rubbed over a whole chicken prior to roasting.

MAKES 2 (HALF-PINT/250 ML) JARS

¼ cup/7 g fresh rosemary leaves
1 cup/190 g finely milled sea salt

Preheat the oven to 200°F/95°C (or lower if you have that option on your oven).

Finely mince the rosemary leaves and combine them in a bowl with the salt. Use your fingertips to rub the rosemary into the salt. Spread the salt mixture on a foil-lined rimmed baking sheet and bake until you can smell the rosemary and the salt feels dry to the touch, about 20 minutes. Remove the pan from the oven and let the salt cool at room temperature. When the salt is cool, break up any chunks that may have formed and pour it into 2 half-pint/250 ml jars. Store in a cool, dark place. It keeps indefinitely, though flavor will diminish after months on the shelf.

HOMEMADE CULTURED BUTTER

CULTURED BUTTER IS MADE FROM CREAM THAT HAS been doctored with beneficial bacteria and allowed to sit at room temperature until it becomes thick and tangy. It used to be that all butter was made from cream that was slightly soured like this, as it frequently took several rounds of milking to gather enough cream to justify a churning session. As refrigeration became widely accessible, it was easier to keep cream from souring and the traditional butter-making techniques were abandoned. In recent years, cultured butter has been rediscovered and is now a specialty item that can cost upwards of $8 a pound.

MAKES 1 (HALF-PINT/250 ML) JAR

1 pint/480 ml heavy cream
2 tablespoons buttermilk
$\frac{1}{4}$ teaspoon fine sea salt

Combine the cream and buttermilk in a jar or bowl and stir until blended. Cover with a tea towel or a piece of cheesecloth and allow it to sit at room temperature for 18 to 36 hours, until it becomes thick and tangy. At this point, you can keep your cultured cream in the refrigerator up to 1 week before you make the butter.

When you're ready to make the butter, pour the thickened cream into the bowl of a food processor. Process until the cream has separated into clumps of butter swimming in liquid, about 2 to 5 minutes.

Place a fine-mesh sieve over a bowl and pour the contents of the food processor bowl through the sieve. Make sure to save the buttermilk you've just created; it's incredibly flavorful and can be used in any recipe that calls for buttermilk.

Using the back of a rubber or silicone spatula, gently move and scrape the butter in the sieve to help remove more of the buttermilk. You will find that a bit of butter pushes through the sieve. Just scrape it off the bottom and plop it back into the sieve.

After you've worked most of the visible buttermilk into the bowl, set the bowl aside. Rinse the butter in the sieve with the coldest water your tap can produce while folding and pressing the butter. The goal is to remove as much of the buttermilk as possible. The more buttermilk you can remove, the longer the shelf life of the butter will be.

After several rinses, place the butter in a shallow bowl and continue to press and (*continued*) fold the butter, still attempting to work any remaining liquid out of the butter. When you feel like the butter has given up as much liquid as it's going to, sprinkle in the sea salt. Mix it into the butter thoroughly with the spatula. In addition to the flavor boost the salt gives, it also extends the shelf life of the butter.

Pack your homemade butter into a wide-mouth half-pint/250 ml jar and store in the refrigerator. It will keep up to 1 week.

HOMEMADE
VANILLA EXTRACT

REAL VANILLA EXTRACT SHOWS UP IN AT LEAST 75 percent of my baking projects. I also like to pour a generous slug into pancake batter and sometimes I make my own honey-sweetened vanilla yogurt. How is it that I'm so free with such a precious commodity? Simple. I make it myself, using bottles of inexpensive vodka and masses of vanilla beans that I buy by the pound online.

MAKES 3 CUPS/720 ML

1 (750 ml) bottle vodka
24 vanilla beans

Pour $\frac{1}{2}$ cup/120 ml vodka from the bottle and reserve.

Split all the vanilla beans and scrape the vanilla seeds from the beans. Using a narrow funnel, push all the vanilla seeds into the bottle of vodka. Cap and shake to distribute. Remove the cap and add the scraped vanilla bean pods to the bottle. Top off the bottle with the reserved vodka (if it all won't quite fit, make yourself a cocktail!) and cap once more. Stash the bottle in a cool, dark place and let it infuse and mellow for 4 to 6 months. You know it's done when the vodka is dark, nearly syrupy, and fragrant with the scent of vanilla. If you have the guts to drink it straight, it should be fairly smooth and deeply vanilla flavored.

If you're keeping the vanilla extract for home use, you can decant some into a smaller bottle for use and then top the bottle off with vodka and vanilla beans to create a bottle of perpetually refreshing extract. If you're making it to give as gifts, you can divide it between smaller jars or bottles (making sure to include at least one or two fresh beans with every gift portion).

CHICKEN STOCK

I FIRMLY BELIEVE THAT CHICKEN WINGS AND FEET make the very best stock, but you can use whatever chicken parts you've got.

MAKES ABOUT 3 TO 4 QUARTS/2.8 TO 3.8 LITERS

3 pounds/1.4 kg chicken parts
3 large carrots, coarsely chopped
1 large onion, quartered
3 celery ribs, coarsely chopped
1 sprig rosemary
1 bay leaf
$\frac{1}{2}$ teaspoon black peppercorns
6 garlic cloves, smashed

Combine all ingredients in the largest pot you have. Cover with 6 quarts/5.7 liters cold water and bring to a boil. Reduce the heat and simmer, uncovered, for 4 to 6 hours, adding more water as necessary to ensure that all chicken parts and vegetables remain submerged. Stock is done when it has taken on a deep, golden hue.

Position a large strainer over another pot and strain the stock. Discard the solids in the strainer.

Return the stock to the heat and bring to a boil. Continue cooking over medium-high heat until the stock has reduced to approximately 3 to 4 quarts/2.8 to 3.8 liters of concentrated stock, approximately 30 to 45 minutes. Pour the stock into any size jars you prefer (I like to have both pints and quarts, as they're both useful), leaving 1 inch/2.5 cm of headroom for the 1-pint/500 ml jars and 2 inches/5 cm for the 1-quart/1 liter jars. Freeze.

When it comes time to use the stock, remove the layer of fat from the surface of the frozen stock before allowing it to defrost.

VEGETABLE STOCK ～⌾

VEGETABLE STOCK IS A GOOD PANTRY STAPLE, PAR-ticularly if you have family members who avoid meat. A couple quarts of homemade veg stock means you're never far away from easy soups and stews.

MAKES ABOUT 3 TO 4 QUARTS/2.8 TO 3.8 LITERS

1 pound/455 g button or cremini mushrooms
4 large carrots, coarsely chopped
1 large onion, quartered
2 leeks, washed well and coarsely chopped
3 celery ribs, coarsely chopped
1 bunch parsley
1 sprig rosemary
1 bay leaf
½ teaspoon black peppercorns
6 garlic cloves, smashed

Combine all ingredients in the largest pot you have. Cover with 6 quarts/5.7 liters cold water and bring to a boil. Reduce the heat and simmer, uncovered, for 4 to 6 hours, adding water as necessary to ensure that all the vegetables remain submerged. Stock is done when the liquid is deeply colored and the vegetables look spent.

Position a large strainer over another pot and strain the stock. Discard the solids in the strainer.

Return the stock to the heat and bring to a boil. Continue cooking over medium-high heat until the stock is reduced to approximately 3 to 4 quarts/2.8 to 3.8 liters of concentrated stock. Pour into any size jars you prefer (I like to have both pints and quarts, as they're both useful), leaving 1 inch/2.5 cm of headroom for the 1-pint/500 ml jars and 2 inches/5 cm for the 1-quart/1 liter jars. Freeze.

FREEZING IN JARS

I know a number of people who have been moving away from using plastic for food storage in recent days. Whether it's out of concern over BPA or simply out of a desire to steer away from petroleum-based products, glass canning jars can be a good alternative to the traditional plastic freezer bags and containers.

The one disadvantage to freezing in glass is that it is not as flexible as plastic, a quality that can occasionally lead to breakage. The trick is to only freeze in wide mouth jar and to leave plenty of headspace when filling the jars. As far as headspace goes, the rule of thumb is to leave a generous inch/2.5 cm per pint/500 ml. This means that pint jars need an inch, while 1-quart/1 liter jars require 2 inches/5 cm.

Much of the food that ends up in jars in my freezer is first frozen on baking sheets. Only when they are frozen solid do I transfer them to jars for longer term storage. When freezing foods like blueberries, grapes and cherry tomatoes, save yourself some grief and make sure to use a rimmed baking sheet. They'll keep those roll-prone foods in place and help prevent a mess. If your baking sheets have gotten a little funky over years of use (like mine), line them with parchment paper prior to setting the fruit on them. These sheets of parchment can be reused through several rounds of freezing, to minimize the waste.

The one true challenge with freezing jars is defrosting. You cannot take a glass jar straight from the freezer and set it in a bowl of warm water to speed defrosting. It will crack (I know—I have done this). The thing to do is to move a frozen jar from freezer to refrigerator, where it can defrost slowly, over the course of hours. It does require a bit more forethought, but you'll get used to that.

Here are some of my favorite freezer items and how I prepare them before putting them in the jars.

STRAWBERRIES

I have found that the very best way to freeze strawberries is to combine them with a bit of sugar, allow their juices to develop, and then freeze them in that sweet liquid. I use 1/2 cup/100 g sugar to every quart/1.4 kg of berries. The easiest way to do this is to wash, hull, and slice the berries (halves or quarters is fine). Pack them into a 1-quart/1 liter jar, leaving about an inch/2.5 cm of space at the top. Pour 1/2 cup/100 g sugar into the jar and shake it around. Let it sit until juicy. Once the berries have relaxed into the sugar, check the amount of headspace. Add more fruit until you have just 2 inches/5 cm of headspace left. Freeze.

I don't recommend freezing strawberries on a baking sheet before storing them in jars, as they have quite a lot of sticky liquid that will eventually transform those individually frozen berries into an unwieldy lump. However, if you cannot cope with freezing your strawberries with sugar and want to freeze them individually, I recommend putting slips of parchment paper between layers of frozen berries, to help prevent a solid mass from forming.

BLUEBERRIES

Blueberries are great because they can be washed, dried, and spread on a rimmed baking sheet to freeze. Once they're frozen, simply transfer them to jars for easy dispensing into bowls of oatmeal or muffin batter. Because you won't be putting the berries into jars until they are frozen, there's no need to leave additional headspace; they've already done all the expanding they'll need to do. You should be able to get approximately 1 pound/455 g of berries into a 1-quart/1 liter jar.

GRAPE TOMATOES

Grape and Sungold tomatoes freeze extremely well. After washing and drying, spill them out on a rimmed baking sheet (just like the blueberries) and freeze until they're solid marbles of tomato goodness. Funnel them into jars once they are frozen. If you care about aesthetics, you can prick each tomato with the tip of your knife before freezing to prevent the skins from cracking. I never bother with that step.

These are great added directly from the freezer to all manner of soups, stews, and pasta sauces.

PEACHES

Don't bother with peeling peaches prior to freezing. Just cut them into eighths and arrange them skin-side down on a rimmed baking sheet. Freeze until solid. Pack frozen peach slices into wide mouth jars, arranging small sheets of parchment paper between every 2 inches/5 cm of peach. This helps prevent the peaches from sticking together while in the freezer.

ZUCCHINI

There's a point during each summer when squash threatens to take over my kitchen. I handle the overflow by freezing it for later batches of quick breads and soups. My preferred method is to grate the zucchini and heap the shreds into a colander, then press to remove water. Measure out cup-size portions (about 125 g) and arrange them on a rimmed baking sheet like little haystacks. Freeze.

Once frozen, layer these zucchini pucks into wide mouth jars, dividing them with slips of parchment paper.

PRESSURE CANNING

When it comes to canning, there are some hard-and-fast rules.
One is that you cannot can low-acid foods in a boiling water bath canner.
When you can a high-acid food product in a boiling water bath, the heat of
the water kills off any microorganisms while the presence of acid prevents
any botulism spores from developing. However, when you don't have those
high levels of acid, there's nothing inside your jar preventing any spores present from growing into botulism. It takes temperatures upwards of
235°F/113°C to kill botulism spores, which is impossible to achieve in a conventional boiling water bath. However, a pressure canner can reach temperatures of 240°F/116°C, which kills the spores and makes your low-acid foods
safe for room temperature storage.

With the exception of the stock recipes in the freezer section and a few other
noted special cases, the recipes in this book have all been developed to be high
enough in acid to be safe for boiling water bath canning. Should you be curious
about dipping a toe into the world of pressure canning, so that you can put up
those low-acid foods in a shelf stable way, I have a few thoughts to share.

First off, don't be afraid of the pressure canner. Truly, it is your friend. Pressure cookers and canners have come a long way from their early days. They've
been designed to be nearly foolproof; it's impossible to remove the lid while the
pressure is up, which eliminates the worry about food exploding in your face.

Second, don't feel like a pressure canner is out of your price range. My 16-
quart Presto canner retails for around $80 these days, which is an investment
that can easily pay off once you start using it. If that feels too steep for you, find
a friend or two to go in on the pot with you. It's not something that you'll use
every day, so it could easily be shared with others.

Do know that pressure canners are different from pressure cookers. Whenever
you're canning under pressure, you must use a pot that has either a weighted or
dial gauge, as knowing the amount of pressure is key to ensuring safety.

Finally, there are some things that just can't be canned at home, even in a pressure canner. Foods containing a great deal of dairy (like chocolate or caramel sauce) as well as thick products like a pumpkin purée just can't be done.

If you are curious about pressure canning and happen to have one in your kitchen, stock is a good item to start with. Here's a primer on how to do it.

Before you get started, make sure to get your pressure canner tested. Even brand-new ones aren't always perfectly accurate, so it's important to take it to a kitchenware store or your local cooperative extension to have your gauge tested. They'll be able to tell you if it reads accurately or if you need to make adjustments in your readings in order to have a safe finished product.

Follow the recipe for either chicken of vegetable stock included in the previous section. If you have the time, refrigerate the stock overnight, so that you can remove any fat before canning.

Place defatted stock in a large pot and bring to a simmer. While it heats, put the necessary number of jars (either pints or quarts) in the pressure canner. Fill the pot with 3 to 4 inches/7.5 to 10 cm of water and put enough water in the jars themselves to keep them from floating. Put the lid on the canner (you don't need to lock it into place at this point) and bring to a boil.

Put the canning lids in a small saucepan and place over very low heat, in order to soften the sealing compound.

When the jars are hot and the stock is simmering, remove one jar from the pot. Empty the water into the sink and carefully fill the jar with stock, leaving a generous 1 inch/2.5 cm of space between the surface of the stock and the top of the jar. Wipe the rim of the jar with a cloth dipped in white vinegar (to help cut any grease), apply a warm lid, and screw on a ring.

Place the filled jar in the pressure canner and repeat the process until all your jars are filled. Put the lid on the pressure canner and lock it into place. Bring the heat up and let the canner run with an open vent for 10 minutes. You want to get as much air out of the canner as possible.

When the stream of steam coming out of the vent starts to reduce, put the vent weight on the port. If you're using a weighted pressure canner, choose the 10 pounds of pressure side of the weight. If you're using a gauged pressure canner, watch your gauge. You need it to reach 11 pounds of pressure (or whatever your canner's equivalent is).

Once the weight is jiggling the appropriate number of times per minute or the gauge has reached 11 pounds of pressure, set a timer for 25 minutes.

Keep tabs on your pot to ensure that the jiggles or gauge number don't drop below their prescribed levels. You may need to reduce the heat to keep the pot where it should be, pressure-wise.

When the time is up, turn the heat off under the pot and let it cool completely before touching. I tend to do my pressure canning right before I go to bed, so that I can leave it to cool all night long.

When the pressure is totally down and the jars are cool enough to handle, remove the jars from the pot. Remove rings and wash jars. The stock often leaks a tiny bit during processing, which can make the jars a little grungy.

Label with the contents and date and store in a cool, dark place. Pressure-canned stock will keep for up to a year on the shelf (although mine never lasts that long).

ACKNOWLEDGMENTS

AS WITH ALL BOOKS, THIS VOLUME YOU'RE HOLDING has been touched and influenced by many hands. My thanks go first to my friend Joy Manning, who connected me to the right people at the very right moment. To my agent, the very no-nonsense Clare Pelino. She has served as guide and coach through this process and I am greatly appreciative for her advice and participation. Thanks also go to my editor, Kristen Green Wiewora, for giving me the opportunity to write the book I'd always imagined and for being such a peach to work with. Steve Legato, thanks for taking such swoon-worthy photos. Amanda Richmond, thanks for making it all look so good on the page.

Of course, my very best readers were my parents, Morris and Leana McClellan. They took my panicked phone calls, talked me through sticky situations, and read every single word of the draft (sometimes twice). I am a lucky girl to have been born to two such good, smart, loving people.

My sister, Raina Rose, has been the world's best jam and granola taster. There's no one in the world who I enjoy feeding more than her. Thanks for letting me heap preserves upon you every time you came to town.

This book wouldn't have happened without the support of my husband, Scott McNulty. His belief in my ability to make my dreams come true is unshakeable. Thanks for letting me fill our apartment with jars, Scotty!

Finally, my thanks go out to the community of canners and bloggers who read, comment, and cook up my creations in their own kitchens. You are the reason I return to the canning pot, season after season.

INDEX

Note: Page references in *italics* indicate photographs.

PRESERVING
NOTES

PRESERVING
NOTES

PRESERVING
NOTES